I0188042

SAM

THE MORNING MAN

by SAM SALERNO

SAM

THE MORNING MAN

by SAM SALERNO

MAY 2017

CARMEL, CALIFORNIA

The words on these pages are the product of a keen memory, a great many files and notes, and my own extemporaneous writing. Every word, expression, and thought in this book is true in fact and meaning as best as I can recall and report.

SAM
THE MORNING MAN

All Rights Reserved
© 2017 by Sam Salerno

No part of this book may be reproduced or transmitted in any form or by any means, electronic or mechanical, including photocopying, recording, or by any information storage and retrieval system, without permission in writing from the publisher.
For permission, please visit **SetonPublishing.com**.

ISBN: 978-0-9989605-0-0

PRINTED IN THE UNITED STATES OF AMERICA

TABLE OF CONTENTS

i Publisher's Note	*43* Lounge Entertainment
iii Introduction	*44* Ocean's Eleven
v Forward	*45* The Rat Pack
vii Acknowledgments	*46* Think Before Speaking
ix About the Author as a Writer	*47* Juice Jobs
	48 MC Chores
PENNSYLVANIA	*50* I'm a Tenor - Not a Baritone
1 The Early Years in Pennsylvania	*51* The Jersey Boys
2 My Dad	*52* The Pen Is Mightier Than The Sword
3 My Mom	*53* The Mormon Influence
	54 Joe Marine
LOS ANGELES	*56* Coffee Time
5 The Celebrities of Belmont High	*57* Broadcasting Around The World
9 Chief of Police of Los Angeles For A Day	*58* Marqee Power
10 If I Knew Then What I Know Now	*59* VIP List
11 My Time In The U.S. Army Air Corps	*62* Covering Sports in Las Vegas
12 They Only Drink For Medicinal Purposes	*63* Four Mile Brothel: A Way to Relieve Tension
	64 Nothing Interfered With Gambling
LAS VEGAS	*65* Hot Spot Near The Strip
13 My Start In Las Vegas	*66* A Great Meeting
14 Cleaning the Cards	*67* A True Story From Cliff Friend
15 Showboat Opening	*68* Interviewing Ella Fitzgerald
16 Transmitter Site	*70* Bob Hope And His Celebrities Play Vegas Golf
17 Al Santoro Writes About Las Vegas	*71* Announcing The Mitch Miller Show
18 Flying In A T-33	*73* Billboard Comes to Las Vegas
19 Gus Giuffre	*74* Good And Fair Competition
20 Meeting George Yardley	*75* The Head Man At The Desert Inn
21 The Chordettes	*76* The Joke Was On Him
23 Vocal Groups	*77* Roy Cohn
24 My 'Brother' Al Alberts	*78* Lowell Thomas
29 Racial Divide	*81* Promoting Record Stars
30 The Night Sammy Davis, Jr. Lost His Eye	*82* Meeting Record Stars
31 Moulin Rouge	*83* Vicki Sallee
32 The Tournament of Champions	*84* Byron Nelson
39 Selling Insurance	*85* One Of The Top Golf Amateurs From Las Vegas
40 Silver Dollars	*86* Liberace
41 Public Relations People	*87* An Invite Every Night
42 The Bag Man	

continued

TABLE OF CONTENTS CONTINUED

103 From The Mouth Of A Babe

104 *Deejay Magazine*

105 Sinatra's *Cristina II*

106 Harry Tobias

107 My Days With Louis Prima

113 Interviewing The Stars

114 Las Vegas Weather

115 Big Band Shows

117 Becoming A Station Manager

118 A Finder's Fee

THE MONTEREY PENINSULA

119 My Children

120 Hang On To Your Hat

122 Tom Sheehy

123 Music In The Barn

124 Herm Edwards

125 Two Broadcasters In College

126 Bill Bates

128 Herb Miller, Glenn's Brothers

129 Monterey's Contribution To Golf

131 Bing Crosby Pro-Am

137 *Play Misty For Me* and KRML

139 Back To You, Jack

140 Broadcast Changes, All About Money

141 He's The King

142 Sports At KMST, Monterey

143 Unforgettable People I've Met

144 Clint Eastwood Invitational Tennis Tournament

147 The Big Three At KRML

148 Emcee For The Night

149 The Day I Knocked A Tree Down In The Spalding

150 Bobby Clampett

151 The Golf Clinic At Pebble Beach

152 Billy Casper

153 Jim Langley

154 Cover Story

155 Eastwood Runs For Mayor Of Carmel

159 A Round Of Golf With Clint Eastwood

160 Some Problems In Publishing

162 Sharing A Microphone With Top Golfers

164 Jerry Douglas

165 First Italian Open

166 *Golf & Tennis West*

167 And All That Jazz

168 Paul Lippman

170 The Strike Zone

171 Willie Mays Sends In A Ringer

172 Producing Magazines

174 Ken Venturi

175 Too Many Snobs

176 Claude Harmon Humor

177 Let Me Go Get The Girls

178 John Madden

179 *The Shagbag Show*

181 Jim Tunney

SOME ADDITIONAL WRITINGS

183 My Writing Years

198 The Pete Rose Debacle

199 No Resemblance To A Real Poet

200 *The Detroit Story*

203 AFTERWORD

205 Books From *setonpublishing.com*

PUBLISHER'S NOTE

When Sam Salerno first called me, he sounded like an old friend, even though we'd never met. Sam has that effect on people, perhaps because he's a man without pretense. Some people learn that life is better lived by being your true self, but I got the feeling that Sam started life that way.

Sam has lived an interesting life, and spent much of it talking with, and writing about, people in the public eye. He got close to people we only know about from the headlines. He's one of those honest journalists who asks the questions we want answered, and he doesn't try to make himself more important than the person he's interviewing. And he's done that on deadline for newspapers and on live radio.

I am pleased to have gotten Sam's story into print, and he made it easy. His professional and courteous attitude made this project even more worthwhile.

Considerable thanks go to Michelle Manos of Michelle Manos Design, who polished the text and did wonders in marrying it with the myriad photos and other visual elements that bring Sam's life story so alive.

Thanks also to Al Estrada who helped to make this book possible.

Tony Seton
CARMEL, CALIFORNIA

INTRODUCTION

I first met Sam Salerno in 2001, when I retired to the small community of Carmel-by-the-Sea in Monterey County, California.

I was immediately impressed with Sam's attitude on life, and his energy and helpful involvement in the community. We both grew up during difficult times for our country - from the '20's to the '50's in the past century - and beyond. The country's values were much different in those days, but we managed to survive to experience unimaginable changes. Our friendship developed from those common experiences that defined our generation.

Sam's continued energy is a mystery considering his stage of life, and for those who know him. He is a living example of longevity enabled by activity. His motto is "Keep moving," and he lives it.

Few octogenarians can compete with his ability to play 18 holes of golf three times a week, as well as to co-host a Saturday morning radio show for the past 14 years… and counting. In addition, he stays active attending various social and business functions while interviewing celebrities for his radio show and periodicals. Sam writes like he talks - without notes or drafts. His words pour out directly from his empirical knowledge, imagination, and an incredible memory for details.

Sam does not dwell on age, and prefers to live a life of activity, rather than sitting around, like some people who worry about the aging process while they vegetate in place.

This country would benefit greatly to consider Sam Salerno a national treasure, and institute a program of scientific study and cloning.

Al Estrada
CARMEL-BY-THE-SEA,OO CALIFORNIA
9 February 2017

FORWARD

All the information and data in this book is factual, based on personal experiences and those relayed to me by close friends and business associates.

It would be incongruous for me to embellish any story or incident that has happened lo these eighty years.

In no way were these stories written to offend anyone, but rather to chronicle part of my career and life. At times, it was problematic to authenticate a name or spelling, because some of those mentioned have passed on, and it was futile to Google them.

One reason I felt I should write this book is to give an accounting of the various jobs and duties I performed in the media. There are many broadcasters and writers who have excelled in only one area of their careers. My career in media ran the entire gamut, from announcing and engineering, to sales and programming management, and to ownership of a radio property. In between, I handled the camera at the Golf Clinic at Pebble Beach, was a marshal at the Spanish Bay Golf Course, wrote for two newspapers on the Monterey Peninsula, and then published my own newspaper for three years.

In addition to all those duties, I raised a family of two boys and two girls. That was the toughest job of all the endeavors, because there were divorces involved, and that's never a happy time.

This book has proven that each of us has a story to tell!

Again, thanks for your interest in my life!

Sam Salerno
CARMEL-BY-THE-SEA, CALIFORNIA
2017

ACKNOWLEDGMENTS

Without the collaboration of Al Estrada, my artist friend in Carmel, and his daughter, Mischa, this book would not have been completed. Their meticulous efforts were immeasurable in organizing and structuring materials, documents, and illustrations; editing photos; and producing the formatted manuscript's digital file.

Settling in the beautiful Monterey Peninsula area was a dream come true. I've acquired many friends here, but space limits me to mentioning only a few. The ones with whom I've spent most memorable times include Clint Eastwood, the late Johnny Adams and Phil Dacey, Dick Buxton, Dave Marzetti, my co-host on the Shag Bag Radio Show, Harold Firstman, Bob Houseman, and the rest of my golfing buddies: Steve King, Bobby Morris, Tom Ballard, Ron Rieser, Bob De Luca, Donnie Blackburn, Bob Sparks, Frank Russo, Elio Chiappe, John Biason, Pat Anderson, Marv Silverman, and Ken Ogletree, Ken Guio, and Dave Anderson.

I would also like to mention Firok Shield, restaurateur extraordinaire, Jim Hogan, the late Joanne Mathewson, and the ever-colorful James Jaurequi. They all encouraged my efforts in their own way, and I am most grateful.

In addition, I would like to acknowledge my gratitude to the many celebrities in the entertainment and golf world whom I've interviewed. They have given of their time and friendship. There are too many to mention here, but they are featured throughout this book.

In Las Vegas, my friends were numerous. They included Abe Fox (Foxy's Deli), Paul Wolfson, Julie Laikin, Al Freeman (Sands Hotel), Gene Murphy (Desert Inn Hotel), Jean McGowan (Dunes Hotel), Lee Fisher (Dunes Hotel), Harvey Diederich (Tropicana Hotel), Abe Schiller (Flamingo Hotel), Maury Stevens (Frontier Hotel), Herb Mac Donald, John Romero (Sahara Hotel), Ralph Mosa, Gene Christian, Jerry Belt, and Joe Marine.

Al Nissel was one of my mentors in Las Vegas. John "Cliff" Friend, the famous song writer who wrote 28 standard tunes, gave me the inspiration to be successful and reminded me to not worry about negative things. His motto was "If you're down, pick yourself up, and always smile." He said, "Things will get better," and they did.

Others who gave me inspiration in school, and in life, included Arnold Sauro, a handsome athlete at Belmont High School in Los Angeles, and Leon Cisin, who first attended radio school in Hollywood and then inspired me to do the same.

I would also like to note that you're never too old to learn how to use a computer. My old typing skills were significantly enhanced by using a computer; it made the writing process flow much more easily. All this enabled me to concentrate on writing the chapters and episodes, and telling my story.

ABOUT THE AUTHOR AS A WRITER

Sam Salerno, the author, was inspired to write this book because of his love for the written word. He was encouraged by his English teachers in Pennsylvania and in Los Angeles. Both teachers, Mrs. Kennedy and Mrs. Hov, thought Sam had the flair and talent for writing. Sam wrote for the school paper at Belmont High in Los Angeles and continued his writing when he attended Monterey Peninsula College in Monterey, California.

During his years in Las Vegas Sam wrote for Panorama Magazine. He was the Las Vegas "stringer" for *Deejay Magazine*, distributed nationwide. When Sam worked for Louis Prima as his publicity director, he wrote all of Louis' press releases for national distribution.

During his years on the Monterey Peninsula, Sam published over 30 tabloids and magazines, principally relating to golf, and in each publication he wrote a story or two. Sam wrote "The Carmel Voice" column for *The Monterey County Post Newspaper* for ten years. He also produced his own newspaper, *The Carmel Voice*, for three years, and in each he wrote the feature story and his own column, "The Carmel Voice."

Along with his writings, Sam produced the Bill Bates cartoon map of Carmel and a 1982 U.S. Open poster as well as a Bing Crosby poster.

PENNSYLVANIA

THE EARLY YEARS IN PENNSYLVANIA

My early years were spent in Bristol, Pennsylvania, a small industrial community located by the Delaware River, between Philadelphia (on the Pennsylvania side) and Trenton (on the New Jersey side). I think the population of the town was around nine or ten thousand.

Our family consisted of my two older sisters, Rose and Anna, and my older brother Frank. My dad worked for the Rohm and Haas Co., a textile firm famous for inventing Plexiglas® which, during World War II, was used exclusively for the noses of the B-17 and B-29 bombers. My dad was a laborer for the company, and after thirty years, he retired from this great company.

I did all the things that young people do: played football and baseball, went sledding, and was as mischievous as any child. My brother Frank was a year older, and his likes and dislikes were entirely different from mine; likewise, for my two sisters. When I was seven years old, my mother gave birth to another sister - Angelina - so then there were five of us.

Dad got tired of shoveling snow, having to weatherproof the home, and walking to work every day. He heard that Rohm and Haas had a factory in South Gate, California, and he headed west. Three months later, the family made the train trip to Southern California. Dad had purchased a home in the Elysian Park area of Los Angeles.

When he came to Los Angeles, Dad remarked, "I should have come out west twenty years sooner!" The rest is history. We loved the area. I went to Belmont High School, as did my brother Frank, and became a Californian.

By the way, the house my father bought cost $2,000. Try to purchase a comparable home today.

When my father, Dominick, came to this county, he was a devout Catholic. He was a smoker, I was told, and drank occasionally, as was the custom with most Italian men who emigrated to the United States.

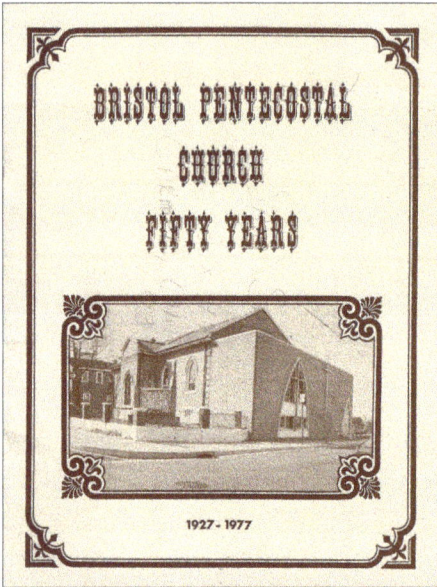

BRISTOL PENTECOSTAL CHURCH FIFTY YEARS

1927 - 1977

After my dad married my mom (Marie), who was from the same part of Italy (Calabria), they converted from their Catholic faith and became 'born again' Christians of the Pentecostal faith.

All of the brothers and sisters were raised like any other children; we didn't know too much about religion. There were many other Italian-Americans who came to the USA and resided in Philadelphia and Bristol and converted, becoming full-fledged Pentecostals.

From the day my dad converted until he suffered his demise at the age of 89, he never swore, drank, smoked, or had a negative word to say about anyone. He was quiet, read the Bible, and went to church regularly. Incidentally, the first Pentecostal church in Bristol was at our home on Dorrance Street. Later the church members built a beautiful church in another part of town.

My dad was quite philosophical for one who wasn't a college grad. About smoking, he said, "If the Lord wanted us to smoke, when he created man he would have had a chimney on his head so the smoke could exit!" When we were doing homework and didn't have a pencil or pen and asked him for one, his reply was, "You go to school and don't even have a pencil!" About work habits, etc., his comment was, "He who sleeps doesn't catch the fish!"

Just a few poignant sayings from the mouth of my Dad. They all make sense today.

My mom was the catalyst for the entire family, a sweet loving person who worked hard at home to keep the peace. She cooked three meals a day, washed the dishes, did the laundry (mostly by hand) for five children, and all the house work (cleaning, mopping, etc.).

Never once did I hear her complain about her work load at home. Mind you, she had four children in succession. In those days there was no such thing as birth control pills. How she handled this burden was a mystery. I guess that's how it was done. Mom also had to intervene when Dad was about to konk us on the head for some mischievous thing we had done. He wasn't very tolerant in that department. Ten hours of labor each day at a factory was not conducive to tolerating any extracurricular activities that we were involved in. His motto was "peace at all times."

When things got rough financially, my mom went to work at one of the local woolen mill factories in Bristol, Pennsylvania. Through it all, she raised five children, and in my mind, she did a wonderful job.

My mom had a great sense of humor and loved to joke. Perhaps I inherited that trait from her. In her later years my mom became a diabetic, and it resulted in her losing her sight. She came to live with me in the 1980's when I leased a house in Carmel. It was tough on me because she needed constant care and I could not afford a full-time nurse for her. Eventually she went back to live with my older sister, Rose, who was living in Groveland, California. I've always been one to honor my parents…after all, we only have one mother and one father. Give them all the love you can because someday, you may be that mother or father!

LOS ANGELES

THE CELEBRITIES OF BELMONT HIGH

I guess every student who has attended a certain high school is proud of some of those from their school who have become famous or popular in various professions.

Belmont High School in Los Angeles was no different, and with Hollywood being so close, many of the Hilltoppers (as our students were known), were part of the cinema crowd, while others made their mark on radio and in comedy.

One of the most popular students who made it big in show biz was Jack Webb, who graduated from Belmont High in the summer class of 1938. Webb was the star of *Dragnet*, the television series, and also starred in some full-fledged motion pictures.

Before Jack Webb, Johnny Bernadino, another

Belmont alumni, went from being a major league baseball player to a regular cast member and star of *General Hospital.* Bernadino played second base for the St. Louis Browns, a major league team that today is the Baltimore Orioles.

While I attended Belmont High, Richard Crenna was a student who played basketball for the senior team, and while in school was a regular on the *Eve Arden Show* and other network productions. Jeff Chandler was also one of the stars. Crenna also starred in the *Rambo* movies with Sylvester Stallone.

One of the first American satirists who ran the political gamut was Mort Sahl, who also attended Belmont High. Sahl and I were in ROTC together, but I wasn't a close friend. I had more of rapport with Crenna.

The most amazing thing about Belmont High is that all of the graduates became successful in their endeavors; doctors, lawyers, teachers, writers, broadcasters, etc., and they attributed their success to the education they got at Belmont. In that era, people went to school to achieve the best education possible. No misfits or trouble makers were tolerated; not like today's environment where all phases must be "politically correct!" Belmont educators never tolerated bad behavior by the students.

R. O. T. C.

FRONT ROW: Cadet Major Dick Mueller, First Lieutenant Niles Davis, First Lieutenant John Vawter.
SECOND ROW: Captain Mort Sahl, Captain Ramon Zarbaugh, Captain Ray Barrier, First Lieutenant Jack Hubbard.

Dick Crenna

HI-Y—Ernest Abrego, Eugene Arellano, John Auchincloss, Gaylord Campbell, Hadley Carrigan, Jim Churchill, Levon Chaloukian, Leon Cisin, Herbert Cooper, Floyd Erickson, Frank Fleming, Jim Flynn, Bill Gillette, Carl Hegge, Joe Hines, Bob Hobbs, Bill Hudson, Donald Jaffe, Bob Johnson, Gordon Millen, Don Mareina, Paul Perkins, Alfred Persson, Harold Rice, Eugene Regan, Sam Salerno, Oakie Shoemaker, Hector Solares, Garry Watson, Don Whitman, Ray Wood, Phil Moore, Willie Quan, Dick Kestell.

Some of the national celebrities who attended Belmont High School in Los Angeles. Upper left, satirist Mort Sahl. On the right, actor Richard Crenna

Youth Takes Over Conduct of City's Affairs for Day

Youngsters Hold Reins as Part of Boys' Week Plan

Don Barrett, a frank, personable senior who yesterday was elevated from the presidency of the student body at Hollywood High School to the position of Los Angeles' chief executive, found one of his first official tasks as Mayor to be the signing of the pay roll.

But, in order to avoid trouble later in the auditing department, the 17-year-old Mayor Barrett judiciously asked the "deposed" Mayor Bowron to countersign.

It was a part of the local observance of Boys' Week.

Occupy Many Positions

Yesterday youths from the city's schools assumed positions in many governmental offices—city, county, State and Federal. They learned firsthand the functions of the various offices and questioned their adult counterparts about the duties and the procedures involved.

In the Council chambers, where 17-year-old Bill Evans of Washington High School presided, the eager, youthful Councilmen debated inconclusively the question of which high school in Los Angeles rates first.

Law enforcement for the day was in the hands of Chief of Police Sam Salerno, 18, president of the student body at Belmont High School, and Sheriff Alex Rados, 16, an Eagle Rock High School senior.

Prosecutor for Day

As District Attorney for the day, Charles Wiggins, 17, of El Monte Union High School, accompanied Dist. Atty. Fred N. Howser to the Peete trial.

George Gonzalez, 17, of Polytechnic High School, was the day's president of the Chamber of Commerce, and Charles Pierce, 18, of Fremont High School, filled the United States Marshal's post.

In Superior Court, Rodney Phillips, 16, of Gardena High School, sat on the bench beside Presiding Judge Samuel R. Blake, and other boy jurists were Gerald Godard, 17, of Torrance, and William Jameson, 17, of Polytechnic High School.

Honors Shared

Salerno, who replaced Chief C. B. Horrall, shared honors at a noon luncheon at the Police Academy with Kenneth Land, 10-year-old 61st Street School lad who received a scroll for his assistance to police in furnishing the license number on the car of the "paper bag" bandit who perpetrated a series of bank robberies in Los Angeles.

Rados, who took over Sheriff Biscailuz's duties as well as his 10-gallon hat and shiny badge, and his 17-year-old undersheriff, James Zwerneman, Whittier High School, played host to some of the other boy officials at lunch in the County Jail.

Fire Chief Edward Johnson, 15-year-old Garfield High School student, and his boy firemen, spent most of the day inspecting Fire Department facilities.

OBSERVANCE PARTICIPANTS—Police Chief Horrall pictured with Sam Salerno, right, and Kenneth Land, left, in Boys' Week observance. Salerno was Chief for a day. Land received scroll for aid in arrest of bandit.

The article that appeared in the *Los Angeles Times* about my position as Chief of Police of Los Angeles, with the real Chief, C.B. Horrall

In the summer of '45 I was elected Student Body President at Belmont High, a great honor for someone who hadn't been in California very long, having made the journey west from Pennsylvania. That same year, my brother Frank was the starting quarterback for Belmont's football team and was a member of all the exclusive clubs at the school.

The competition was keen when I ran for office, and my opponents were as popular and well-liked as I was. Raymond Wood was a track star, tall, blond, and good looking. Bill Gillette was the guy the girls went "gaga" over; he was a good student and a basketball player who later went to UCLA and became a teacher. My final opponent was a fellow named Fred Speigl, whose family moved to the United States to escape Hitler's wrath against the Jews. He too was a scholar and a tough competitor.

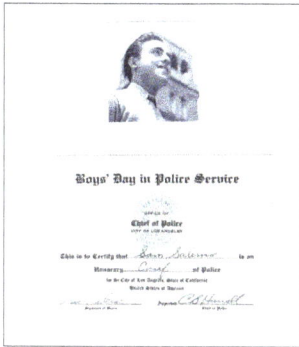

I think the secret of my victory over all of my opponents was my relationship with all the students, regardless of their ethnicity. I knew everyone and made sure I gave them my time, even before the election took place. We had people of every imaginable ancestry –Mexican, Chinese, African, and more – so it behooved me to befriend all of them during my years at Belmont.

I won the election by what margin I don't recall, but I was happy as were those who believed in me.

During my tenure, I was given the honor of being the Chief of Police of Los Angeles for one day, filling in for C.B. Horrall, the Acting Chief. Other student body presidents were given other positions; Sheriff, D.A., etc. Again, I was happy at the time, but looking back at all this attention I was getting then, it was mind-boggling. Such was the life of an 18-year-old in 1945.

I have always been one who seems to be ahead of the times, and I will relate a couple of incidents that perhaps make it seem that I am psychic.

In high school in Los Angeles, we had our share of characters; some were athletes, others scholars, and the rest just plain old folks. One of the characters I wrote about then was a fellow named George Nichols. He was of Russian extraction, and I believe his parents changed their name when they came to America, which was the case of many who had large names and didn't sound "American." Their real name was Nickaloff, and I presume that's why they changed it. He was a real character, as were Arnold Sauro, Johnny Hahn (who attended Cathedral High, a Catholic school), Ziggy Ringwald, and Leon Cisin.

I gave George Nichols the name "Jacob Schreck" and wrote a little parody at the time. It went like this:

Against the thrusts of the passing winds, into valleys of forgotten sin…
across the plains that saw no time, our boy Jacob was sure to shine.

Now the reason I mention the Schreck is the fact that a movie came out in 2001 called *Shrek*. Who would have thought that in 1945 I would create a name that was similar to a hit movie. So it goes.

Another similar happening took place when Greg Norman was the top golfer in the world and came to the Monterey Peninsula to play in the Spalding Pro-Am. I published the official magazine for Harold Firstman, the promoter of the tournament. In the magazine I wrote a story of Norman and called it *Shark Attack*. Well, a year after I wrote the story, Greg Norman and George Pieper of *Golf Magazine* combined to write a booked called *Shark Attack*. No, I didn't sue, but it gives you some idea of what can happen after you create something early but don't follow up and others do, and make money with your idea.

So, if you have an idea or a creation, jump on it, and don't wait, because others are lurking to capitalize on your idea.

MY TIME IN THE U.S. ARMY AIR CORPS

I received my notice to begin serving in the United States Army in June of 1945. My orders were to report on July 2, 1945 to Fort McArthur in San Pedro, California. World War II was still in progress and no signs of it being over. The European skirmish was scaling down, but the Pacific War was hot and heavy, still in progress.

At San Pedro, an exam from the Army doctors confirmed that I had flat feet. Thus, I was of no service to them as a foot soldier. The Army transferred me to the Army Air Corps, and I began boot camp at Sheppard Field, Wichita Falls, Texas.

After training, I was sent to Scott Field, Illinois, for six months of radio training, transmitting Morse code on aircraft radio equipment.

Upon graduation, the war was coming to an end in both theaters of operation, and my skills were not needed; likewise for those who graduated with me. About fifteen soldiers began the course, and only five lasted 'til the end.

I enjoyed all the buddies I became acquainted with from every town, city, and state in this great country. We were all young and naive and didn't know much at the time.

From Scott Field I was sent to Langley Field, Virginia; then to Jackson, Mississippi. From there, I spent some time at Maxwell Field in Montgomery, Alabama.

The war ended, and I was given an honorable discharge. A few officers begged me to stay in and assured me I would be sent to Officer Candidate School, but my mind was made up to once again become a civilian.

My time in the service gave me my G.I. Bill to attend school and still offers me a good deal of medical services.

When I attended the Don Martin School of Radio Arts in Hollywood, we had a group of guys bent on making their marks in the broadcast world. One of the features of this great school was their placement record for graduates. Jobs were available in many locales. My first broadcast experience was in Fort Bragg, California, a town known for fish and lumber. The prime employer in this Northern California town was the Union Lumber Company, responsible for producing lumber for the nation and some countries abroad.

I spent a total of six months in Fort Bragg and made many friends, most of whom were part of Finnish families, and were fisherman. The Portuguese and Italians, along with the Russians, were also part of the fishing community. My boss and owner of KDAC was a Bohemian by the name of Ed Mertle, who also was proprietor of the Welcome Inn, a restaurant-bar in downtown Fort Bragg.

Chuck Gropp, one of my buddies who was at school with me in Hollywood, went to Salt Lake City for his first radio gig at Radio Station KNAK.

After we had been on our respective jobs for six months, we met in Los Angeles and started conversing about our experiences as novices in the profession. I told Chuck about Fort Bragg and the interesting ethnic groups who make up the population and their idiosyncrasies. He began to tell me about Salt Lake City and the Mormon population who dominated every facet of that society.

Being ignorant about what they were all about I asked Chuck about the Mormons. He told me that they are very religious, didn't smoke, and only drank for medicinal purposes. He said, in a joking way, "You know, Sam, there are a lot of sick Mormons there!"

This was quite a coincidence, because later in life, I married a gal whose family practiced the Mormon faith.

ON THE AIR

3

LAS VEGAS

MY START IN LAS VEGAS

I never would have imagined what gambling was all about or what adventures were in store for this novice broadcaster heading for "Sin City," "Glitter Gulch," and all the other names that were synonymous with Las Vegas.

I was driving on Highway 15 heading for Las Vegas to audition for a radio broadcasting job at radio station KRAM, located in the Flamingo Hotel. The year was 1953, and even though I grew up in Los Angeles, I knew nothing about Las Vegas, nor did I know anything about gambling.

The Flamingo Hotel was, if you'll pardon the expression, the last resort on the Las Vegas Strip. One could traverse Las Vegas Boulevard by auto from that hotel to downtown Las Vegas in less than ten minutes. *Try that today!*

Martin Black, one of the early media celebrities in Las Vegas, was the program director at KRAM, and I was to audition for him. The owners of KRAM were Ed Jansen and Truman Hinkle. Both were solid citizens and knew their craft well.

The studios of KRAM were in the rear of the Flamingo Hotel near the swimming pool. The station was affiliated with the Mutual Network, carrying their hourly news reports and some half-hour drama shows, most of which were taped and re-played during the 8 to 9 p.m. segment.

I won the audition from among a group of new radio broadcasters who were as young and innocent as I was. My disc-jockey stint emanated from the transmitter site located close to North Las Vegas and near Cashman Field. Baseball games and other events were held year-round at this ball field.

My hours were filled playing the top artists of the day – Sinatra, Como, Presley, The Four Lads, The Four Aces, etc. It was a middle-of-the road format – MOR in radio jargon – interspersed with Mutual News on the hour.

At night one of the features was a formatted show (by the ad agency, McCann-Erickson) called *Lucky Lager Dance Time*. The show was featured in about 20 or 30 radio markets around the country, and all the hit tunes of the day were included in the format.

CLEANING THE CARDS

When it came to gambling, I didn't know anything; I had no clue. After all, I was in my early 20's, came from a religious family, and knew only about sports.

I was walking through one of the hotels and casino and saw these two women at what appeared to be a card table (such as 21). They were moving the cards back and forth across the cloth surface. I pondered and said to myself, "What kind of a game is this?"

The women continued moving the cards, similar to a séance. There was no one sitting at the 21 table, so I was perplexed.

Curiosity got the best of me, so I asked one of the women what game they were playing. They snickered and remarked that it wasn't a card game of any kind…they simply were "cleaning the cards."

In those days, the hotels were more frugal than they are today. When a dealer feels the cards have had their day, they'll deal with a brand new pack. The old one is simply discarded! This procedure is similar to major league baseball when a pitcher demands a new ball when the one he is using is scuffed.

Wow - I thought the girls invented a new game.

Let's call it naiveté on my part.

HISTORY ON TAPE — Ruby Kolod, (second from left), Casino Manager of the Showboat, accepts a taped recording of opening day ceremonies held at the Showboat from Fred Young, Chief Engineer of Radio Station KRAM, as Les Seiffer, Commercial Manager of KRAM, Bill Friday, Operations Manager of Showboat and Sam Salerno, Program Director of KRAM look on. Tape will be placed in "ship's hold" at the Boulder Highway enterprise.

In the early '50's there was always something eventful happening in Las Vegas, from hotel openings to new stars being featured on the Strip. As program director of KRAM with studios in the Flamingo Hotel, I was called upon to be master of ceremonies on many occasions.

The commercial manager of KRAM was Les Seiffer. One of his accounts was the Showboat Hotel, which was located at the beginning of the Boulder Highway, the road that led to Henderson and Lake Mead. The Showboat, in addition to being a top-notch casino, also had a bowling alley that was second to none. Many nationally-televised tournaments emanated from that location. It was quite popular with bowlers who visited Las Vegas.

When the Showboat opened, Les got the idea, and it was approved by casino manager, Ruby Kolod, to make a recording that would last in perpetuity. It would be buried in the ship's hold.

The tape idea would be historical and would be another feather in my broadcasting cap. At the time, I didn't think much of it, but in later years I was proud to have been chosen to have my voice recorded and buried for the ages. The recording chores were handled by KRAM's chief engineer, Fred Young. Fred also filled in at times as a temporary disc jockey.

I haven't been back to Las Vegas, but I've heard that the Showboat Hotel does not exist…that it was torn down. If it is true, my question is, "What happened to the tape?"

So much for history.

TRANSMITTER SITE

In the early days of radio, smaller markets employed "combo men," those who were announcers and during their dee jay stint could also record the transmitter readings each hour to adhere to Federal Communications Commission rules. These dee jays were considered engineers because they possessed a first-class phone license. The majority of the combo men would electrocute themselves if they actually attempted to solve an engineering problem.

If it was a difficult problem, and they couldn't kick the transmitter back on when it failed, they would call the *real* engineer, who would come post-haste to fix the problem.

In major markets (New York, Los Angeles, Chicago, etc.) you were either an engineer or a dee jay. The unions forbade an announcer to touch the equipment.

What brought all this to mind was my work at the KRAM transmitter site during the night stint, where I hosted the *Lucky Lager Dance Time*. As I noted earlier, the transmitter for the station was located north of town near Cashman Field, and the roads up there were unpaved.

All the dee jays had their groupies, and I was no exception. One woman in particular who had the hots for me came to the transmitter site one night as I spun the records. I had been seeing her on a regular basis. So you get the full picture - mink coats and stoles were the norm for women in Las Vegas during the '50's and '60's. Today people dress differently when going for a night out, whether it's Vegas or any other locale.

Anyway, it began to rain in buckets, and there was no way she could walk to her car, which was in a virtual quagmire. So when I signed off for the night, I decided to carry her to her car. Perhaps at that moment I must have thought I was Superman, because she was no lightweight, and really too much for me to carry any distance. We made it for about fifteen yards, and the inevitable happened. We both fell to the ground in the muck and mire, laughing hysterically.

That night, the dry cleaner was the only one who made out!

In the early '50's one of the top sports writers in the Los Angeles area was Al Santoro. His column was featured in the *Los Angeles Examiner.*

That was the year I arrived in Las Vegas to begin my radio career and, in addition, I wrote a little. Some commercials, and some short stories - particularly sports-oriented items.

Las Vegas High School's football team was one of the best in the entire country, and we were all proud of their exploits on the gridiron. The Los Angeles folks were unaware how good Las Vegas' team really was, so I took it upon myself to let the Angelenos know what was happening in Sin City. After all, Las Vegas High was undefeated and had scored 308 points to the opponent's 26 points, so this was worthy of a good deal of 'ink,' as the saying goes.

In addition to winning games in the league and in their conference, Las Vegas took on the big boys from Arizona (Prescott), Utah (Dixie), Phoenix (St. Mary's), Compton, and Pasadena, defeating them handily. It was a year like I've never seen before in high school football. Las Vegas High was dominant in every aspect of the game.

2—Sec. IV Wed., Nov. 18, 1953 **Los Angeles Examiner**

To the Point—
Bruins Figure to Win by One Length
—By Al Santoro—
Sports Editor

BRUINS BY ONE LENGTH: If you figure these football games by the figures, like the men who do horse arithmetic, you must figure the Bruins to beat the Trojans by one length. Bruins' rushing average 247.5, Trojans 188.9; pass offense, Trojans percentage .451, UCLA, .403; total offense, Bruins 311.4 average, Trojans 289.1; interceptions two touchdowns each; punt returns, Trojans 11.1, Bruins 10.8; kickoff returns, Trojans 20.4 average, Bruins 18.4; rushing defense, Trojans 114.5 average, Bruins 118.8; Pass defense Bruins .476, Trojans 447; Total defense Bruins 198.4, Trojans 240.7. No more than a length, but possibly a dead-heat . . . Stanford, we believe, by three lengths.

* * *

. . . Las Vegas High School is undefeated, 308 points scored against only 26 for opponents. Sam Salerno of KRAM sends along the record: Vegas 71, Dixie (Utah), 0; Vegas 52, Basic (Nevada), 7; Vegas 27, Prescott (Arizona), 0; Vegas 13, Compton, 6; Vegas 6, Colton, 0; Vegas 14, Anaheim, 7; Vegas 18, St. Mary's (Phoenix) 6; Vegas 48, White Pine (Ely, Nev.), 0; Vegas 25, Pasadena High, 0; Vegas 34, Reno High, 0.

"Until Ken Fujii, Reno, ran 48 yards against Vegas, longest run in nine games was 26 yards. Fans here say this year's squad best ever assembled, thanks to Coach Angelo Collis. College scouts from Utah and Arizona say Tackle Fred Leavitt is team's outstanding college prospect; Quarterback Johnny Demman completed 42 passes in 87 attempts—some 50 and 60 yards."

The coach that year was Angelo Collis and he had college scouts checking out the team at every game.

It was nice to have Santoro mention the team in one of his columns; it made the school and players happy. After all, Las Vegas wasn't densely populated in those days, and for a small school to get this kind of recognition, it was the talk of the town.

Now, with the massive influx of people, Las Vegas has many schools for the kids to attend. In the '50's I can remember just three schools - Las Vegas High, Gorman High, and Rancho High School. Then it was a small community and now, it's a metropolis.

There were many perks being a disc jockey in Las Vegas in the early '50's and '60's.

We of the Fourth Estate were invited to new hotel openings, new restaurants, sporting events, new show openings, and other events. Those promoting their venues always needed help from the media.

Not only was Las Vegas famous for its hotels and shows; it was also the home of the famous U.S. Air Force Thunderbirds stationed at Nellis Air Force Base.

To help promote the Thunderbird pilots and their exploits, Nellis decided to invite some of the local celebrities (media folk) to take a flight in a jet plane. Well, having flown in the Air Force as a private, I accepted their offer to take a flight. These were T-33 jet trainers, two-seaters with pilot in the rear and passenger in the front.

I can't recall the pilot's name, but with full Air Force gear I went up with this experienced flyer. Prior to take off, I was asked what maneuvers I wanted him to perform, to which I answered, "Give me the works!"

Well, the flight was stupendous, and the pilot performed every maneuver, possibly hitting a few G's here and there. Surprisingly, I didn't lose my food leaving the cockpit, but I was a little woozy after the flight.

I complimented the pilot and expounded on this experience on my radio show the next morning.

The military is more cautious of these events today because of potential lawsuits in case of an accident or some disaster with a media person.

The flight is something I'll cherish for life.

Go Air Force!

GUS GIUFFRE

One of the most popular personalities to make his impact on Las Vegas was Gus Giuffre. He arrived in Las Vegas at the beginning of 1953, the same time I did.

Gus made the trek from Indianapolis, where he was employed as a fireman. He had a great voice, which in those days was mandatory in the radio field. Today, 'voice' is not that important; it's content that counts, and not the quality of your voice. Too bad it's changed.

Gus was a jock on KRAM with studios in the Flamingo Hotel; he was on during the early afternoon hours. I followed his show on that station. His family was most important to him, and they came west after he secured a job and made enough to rent a house. Prior to their arrival and securing a residence for them, he lived in his Nash Rambler. Talk about things being rough.

Once when his wife was ill and he couldn't get quick medical help from the doctors in Las Vegas, he blasted them on his radio show. He called them hypocrites and tied his criticism with the Hippocratic Oath they take when they get their medical degrees. This was Gus, and he never changed his thoughts or opinions when he felt he was right on a topic or situation.

Gus left radio and ventured into the TV world. He moved over to KSHO-TV to host a nightly movie show. Again, his popularity soared. Many of the Strip hotel stars were regulars on his show and appeared with him often. He also was master of ceremonies for a number of big events in Sin City.

Anyone who lived in Las Vegas from 1953 to 1968 knew Gus Giuffre and liked his shows and interviews. He was one of the good guys in broadcasting.

When I purchased KRML in 1968, Gus was one of the first friends to congratulate me and wish me well in my new endeavor.

The Desert Inn Country Club was site of the Tournament of Champions and a great venue for many other golf outings for celebrities and others. When an important golfer came to town, he insisted on playing 18 at the D.I., as it was known.

Art Bruno and his brother Al came to town to visit this reporter and disc jockey, and they wanted to play the course. The Bruno family members were close friends of mine, and I made sure they experienced a round at the Desert Inn Country Club.

Both had caddied at Cypress Point and Pebble Beach, so they were no schlocks when it came to hitting a golf ball.

Art shot even par 72 and brother Al went for 80 blows. After the round, Art remarked, "This is no golf course. It's more like a tennis court. We have golf courses on the Peninsula." End of that story.

TAKING A BREATHER—Taking a breather after a round of golf at the Desert Inn Country Club recently were (l to r) George Yardley, pro basketball star with the Syracuse Nationals; Dick Gibson, secretary of the California Golf Association; Bob Fowler, recreation director at Nevada Test Site, and Sam Salerno, Las Vegas radio personality. Yardley and Gibson were guests of honor at the second annual awards dinner for Nevada Test Site personnel, Salerno was master of ceremonies and Fowler was coordinator of the event.

A celebrity who came to town after his NBA season with the Syracuse Nationals of the National Basketball Association was George Yardley, a tall man at that particular time. In today's NBA line up, he would be just an average player from a height standpoint. He was a good golfer, as are many of today's athletes.

The golf outing was handled by Bob Fowler, recreation director of the Nevada Test Site, and in our foursome, Dick Gibson, Secretary of the California Golf Association, joined the fray.

I was on hand at the Desert Inn because I was master of ceremonies for the second annual awards dinner for Nevada Test Site personnel.

To this day, I haven't experienced any radiation from the likes of Bob Fowler. This was the period when the U.S. Government was testing the Atomic Bomb at Mercury, Nevada, some 70 miles from Las Vegas.

After I left radio school in Hollywood and worked a couple of radio jobs in Fort Bragg and Monterey, California, it was a surprised to be surrounded by a good deal of talent entertaining on the Las Vegas Strip. I was kind of a greenhorn, because at my two previous jobs interviews with show folks or sports, personalities were out of the question.

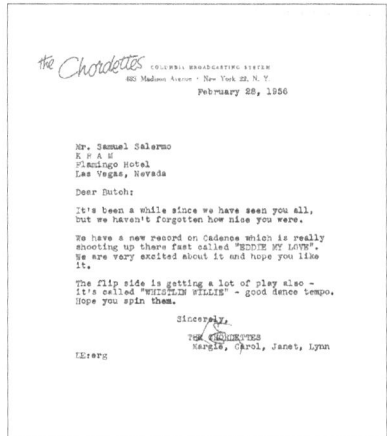

The publicity magnates on the Strip made sure that all the deejays, particularly those with the largest audiences, had access to the stars, whether they were comics, soloists, or musical groups.

The Four Knights were on my show, as were the Lancers, The Four Lads, The Chuck Leonard Quartet, and many others during the early radio days in Las Vegas. At that time, the music charts were airing a tune called *Mr. Sandman,* recorded by four beautiful women called the Chordettes. Their records were featured on the Cadence Label, and their orchestra leader was Archie Bleyer. I don't know the figure, but I think the record went gold within the first few months of its airing.

Was I surprised when I was told they were coming on my show! Not only were they talented, but they were enjoyable to be around, and glib when it came time to share a microphone. It certainly makes the deejay's job a lot easier when those you interview are not bashful about conversing. After the interview, we did some socializing with the girls. They didn't have to worry about my spinning their hit record, or other songs featured in their album.

Chatting with the Chordettes was one of the highlights of my Vegas experience in broadcasting.

I think the feeling was mutual on their part.

VOCAL GROUPS

Today, there aren't as many vocal groups making stage appearances, nor are they recording as they were when I first started in broadcasting. Quite a few rock groups are recording, but vocal duets, trios, and quartets are not releasing new music as they were, at least in my observation.

Some of the hottest recording groups whose records I spun were The Four Aces, The Four Lads, The Hilltoppers, The Four Freshman, The Lettermen, The Four Knights, The Lancers, The Four Tunes, Bill Haley and his Comets, and the Hi-Lo's. Each group had its own distinctive sound and style, and they emphasized it on records and in personal appearances.

It was always great to communicate with these groups on both a personal level and professionally. They were ordinary people just like you and me, but they had musical talents that most of us never had. If the radio station was missing their product, a call or a letter would get you their latest recording. It was wise on their part to furnish disc jockeys the material. It made for million sellers in many cases by providing total exposure in the proper markets.

One member of the Lancers, Corky Lingren, their basso, was not only a friend, but he also taught at the Don Martin School of Radio Arts in Hollywood, the school I attended to learn all the facets of broadcasting.

The Chuck Leonard Quartet and the Salmas Brothers were two groups we befriended during the Vegas years. I can't say that any group had an attitude, and all were friendly toward the deejays.

Some of the groups mentioned are still singing today, and you can hear them through iTunes and other Internet sources.

During their reign as one of the best vocal groups in the country, the Four Aces frequented our studios for conversation, mostly about their latest single and long playing record releases. Al Alberts was their lead singer and the spokesperson for the group.

The Four Aces all came from the Philadelphia area, which was no surprise, because during that era of music that city produced a great many musicians and vocalists like Eddie Fisher, Fabian, Frankie Avalon, and Sunny Gale, to name a few.

There were some listeners who called to tell me that I resembled Al Alberts in appearance, so when I introduced the group on air, I would say, "Here are the Four Aces, featuring my brother Al Alberts." Would you believe, some folks thought it was the truth. So the ploy lasted as long as their records were played.

In addition to my "brother," the Four Aces consisted of Sod Vaccaro, Lou Silvestri, and Dave Mahoney. Whenever they were on the road, whether in the States or abroad, they would keep me posted on where they were appearing, and what was happening with their recordings.

One of their biggest hits was *Love Is a Many Splendored Thing*, which was number one on the charts for a good period of time.

When he married and had a child, Al disbanded the group and was doing solo on singles and LP's.

BILL HALEY And His COMETS   Personal Direction   Exclusive Booking Direction
Decca Recording Artists   JAMES H. FERGUSON   JOLLY JOYCE Agency

The FOUR TUNES

RAY CONNIFF
17348 WEDDINGTON STREET
ENCINO, CALIFORNIA

May 28, 1959

Mr. Sam Salerno
1390 S. 8th
Las Vegas, Nevada

Dear Sam,

Thank you for your letter of
May 25.

I am sending under separate
cover two copies of Hollywood in
Rhythm. One to you personally, the
other to the gang at KLAS.

I have noted the change of
address on my D.J. book.

Best regards,

Ray Conniff

RC:gr

RAY CONNIFF
103 LUQUER ROAD
PORT WASHINGTON, NEW YORK

August 12, 1958

Dear Sam:

Just a note to tell you how nice it was meeting
you on my recent trip through Las Vegas. I am
proud to say that we left your fair city $600.00
richer than when we came. Not bad for amateurs!

Thanks again for all the help you have given me
in the past, and if there is anything I can do,
please don't hesitate to call on me.

Best regards,

Ray Conniff

RC:ab

HERB KESSLER
Personal Manager

THE FOUR ACES
Decca Recording Artists

MCA ARTISTS LTD

BOAR LANE AND GENERAL POST OFFICE, LEEDS

CHADWICK STUDIO PRODUCTIONS

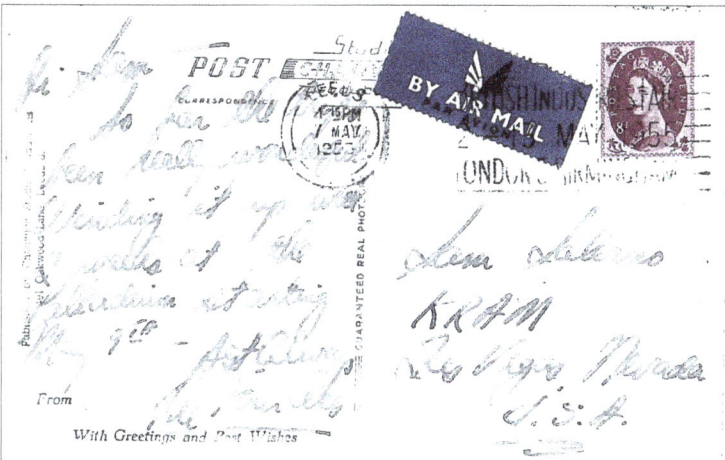

POST CARD

CORRESPONDENCE

BY AIR MAIL

From

With Greetings and Best Wishes

Letter 1 (top left)

FREEMAN COMPANY
PUBLIC RELATIONS

6/13

Dear Sam,

We had so much fun with you guys and Rosemary Clooney that I'd
like to repeat it with Peter Lind Hayes and Mary Healy, and
invite all the boys and their wives in for dinner this Thursday
night, June 16. Please let me know if you can make it, and the
table will be listed under the title "Disc Jockeys".

I wonder if you could help us out with the Las Vegas Police Benefit
Show next Monday, by talking up the show between now and then?
We need lots of help to sell enough tickets to make this a
successful affair, and I am sure the police officers and myself
would really appreciate all the pounding you can give your
listeners about it. Here's the info:

It's the 9th annual police show, at Cashman Field, Monday June 20,
starting at 8:30 p.m. Stars who will perform are Louis Prima and
his outfit, Louis Jordan and his outfit, Mary Kaye Trio, The
Treniers, Kitty Kallen, Mickey Rooney, Kay Starr, Sammy Davis, Jr.,
Peter Lind Hayes and Mary Healy with the entire CopaGirl line,
Abbe Lane, Xavier Cugat, Anna Maria Alberghetti, Gordon MacRae,
and the show will be played by Antonio Morelli and the Sands
orchestra.

In addition, the crowning of the police queen will be done by
Vera-Ellen and the special first Sgt. Robert Dula Sportsmanship
Award will be presented by Jou Louis and Noel Coward to 2 Las Vegas
youngsters for the most outstanding act of heroism, sacrifice, or
sportsmanship in the past year. The Sgt. Dula Award will be an
annual award and the news of the winners will not be announced until
the presentation is made the night of the benefit after the stars
have performed.

Tickets are on sale through any police officer or sheriff's deputy
and are $1, $2 and $5. I would really appreciate it if you will
pound this home during the coming week.

Kindest regards.

Al freeman

BEVERLY HILLS, CAL. · 445 SOUTH BEVERLY DRIVE · CRESTVIEW 4-2024

Letter 2 (top right)

SPIN THE RECORD!!!

TREND RECORDS, INC.
680 NORTH SEPULVEDA BOULEVARD · ARIZONA 8-4203 · 7-2117
LOS ANGELES 49 CALIFORNIA

Friday Eve—
Feb. 25, 1954

Sammy-boy!

I'm lookin' at the wonderful
response you sent Trend via card re
Reg O'Neil — & thinkin' what a nice
card it was — & what a nice guy
you are ...... to overlook our manifold
faults & to like us, in spite of them.
Three weeks ago, with Eartha Kitt
headlining, the owner of this club (Harry Alt-
man) said we were stopping the show &
could we come back as headliners in three
weeks' time, the quickest return-booking in
Town Casino history! We were able to cancel
the Detroit date, so, here we are — having
a ball. After 5 days at Woodhurst Country
club, Hewel — we return home, & on or about
May 1st, we debut in New York City at La Vie
en Rose. Meanwhile, we hope to be seeing
you in April, perhaps. Good luck, pal — Corky

Letter 3 (bottom left)

The Sands

HIGHWAY 91 · LAS VEGAS, NEVADA · TELEPHONE 7100

July 19, 1955

Mr. Sam Salerno
KRAM
Las Vegas, Nevada

Dear Sam:

I am sending you a record by Helen O'Connell
on which she sings two of the songs you saw
produced on The Sands stage in the recent
ZIEGFELD FOLLIES, and would appreciate your
giving this a spin.

With kindest regards.

Sincerely,

Jack

JACK ENTRATTER

JE:ER
Enc.

a place in the sun

Letter 4 (bottom right)

The CREW-CUTS

1008 HIPPODROME BLDG.
CLEVELAND 14, OHIO
CHerry 1-3713

March 12th, 1955

Mr. Sam Salerno
Station KRAM
Las Vegas, Nev.

Dear Sam:

Just a little reminder that the
CREW-CUTS will be at El Rancho Vegas thru March 29th.
We certainly hope you'll have a chance to stop by
to see the boys again. Just call me anytime for
reservations.

On coming Saturday, March 19th,
at Ruth Howard's Record Center, the CREW-CUTS will
have an autograph session starting at 3 PM. We'd
certainly like to have you come down and maybe you
could ask your listeners to come down, too.

Best personal regards.

Sincerely,

Fred

Fred Strauss.

FS/as

JOHNNIE PERKINS · RUDI MAUGERI · PAT BARRETT · RAY PERKINS

Little did I realize there was a 'color thing' in Las Vegas; that is, Blacks were not allowed to patronize the Strip hotels and the downtown casinos. What brought this to light was when I invited my friends, The Four Knights, who had a big hit record on Capitol called *Oh Happy Day*. They were appearing at the El Cortez Hotel in downtown Las Vegas. After one of their sessions (the last for the night), I suggested we go to the Golden Nugget on Fremont Street for a drink.

One of the Knights, Claire Dixon, said to me, "Sam, I don't think they'll serve us because we're Black." I thought he was wrong, but what did this naive disc-jockey know? Well, we went to the Nugget and sat there for one hour. Dixon was correct; They just looked at us with disdain, and no service was extended our way. We left the casino in disgust. This was my first taste of racial discrimination. (The other members of the Knights were Gene Alford and Oscar Broadway, their basso.)

Frank Sinatra was responsible for breaking the color line in the gaming town. Sinatra, who drew the high rollers when he appeared at the Sands Hotel, told the bigwigs that if Sammy Davis, Jr. and Nat King Cole could not stay at the hotel, he's out of there, and would not come back to Las Vegas. Well, the rest is history. And thank God for that. So Blacks owe a debt of gratitude for Sinatra's stand against the Vegas hotels and their attitude toward those of color.

Another popular group seen and heard at the El Cortez Hotel was Bill Haley and his Comets, who capitalized on their big hit *Rock Around The Clock*.

Incidentally, when I was student president at Belmont High School, I turned over the gavel to the next president, Joe Hines, a Black student and a great athlete. We knew nothing of discrimination.

THE NIGHT SAMMY DAVIS, JR. LOST HIS EYE

The members of the media (radio, newspaper, and TV personalities) were invited to the opening of the Will Masten Trio, featuring Sammy Davis, Jr. at the Old Frontier Hotel on the Las Vegas Strip. We members of the press were really looking forward to that big night in the early '50's. Sammy Davis, Jr. and recordings with his vocal interpretations of other singers, and also his ability to dance and play numerous instruments, including the drums, was the talk of show biz.

The early dinner shows usually started at 8 p.m. , and we arrived at 7 so we could drink and dine. Hotels never enjoyed serving, nor did the entertainers, while the show was in progress. We had a great dinner, usually a martini, then a filet mignon, with a tasty dessert to complete the meal.

The curtain was closed, and we were all fidgety, awaiting the announcement that Sammy Davis, Jr. would appear with the Will Mastin Trio.

I can't recall whether the band behind the curtain played a fanfare, but walking through the curtain opening came actor Jeff Chandler, who was famous in films and on network radio (*Our Miss Brooks*). Jeff grabbed the microphone and informed all in attendance that Sammy Davis, Jr. would not appear that night because he was in a major auto accident on his way back to Las Vegas. Everyone was stunned to hear this depressing news.

In the accident, from which he otherwise fully recovered, Sammy lost an eye. He wore a glass eye the rest of his career, which never faltered after the accident.

The Will Masten Trio disbanded, but Sammy Davis, Jr. carved his niche in film and personal appearances. He was an integral part of the famous 'Rat Pack.'

MOULIN ROUGE

During the heyday of Las Vegas and the Strip hotels (early '50's), someone got the brainstorm that it would be profitable to open a casino on the west side of Las Vegas; that is the 'black' area of the city. Most of those living in that area were working at the hotels. Few were professionals in any facet of Las Vegas society. Later, of course, that changed, much to the delight of all.

I thought it was a stupid idea to build a hotel-casino in that part of town. Regular Strip patrons would not go because it wouldn't be productive to venture into that part of town. Conversely, the Blacks were not your big spenders because of their income, and it had only been a short period that they had been welcomed on the Las Vegas Strip.

Nonetheless, a beautiful hotel called the Moulin Rouge was erected with all the amenities of a Strip hotel. If you closed your eyes and opened them, you would have thought you were on the Las Vegas Strip.

I went to the Moulin Rouge with my German girlfriend, Inge, to see and interview Satchmo Louis Armstrong for my radio show. Louis was congenial and quite interesting to chat with.

As predicted, the Moulin Rouge didn't last long, because the high rollers would not bring their action to this part of town. It was too far off the beaten path, geographically and culturally. When gamblers came to Las Vegas, they wanted to be at a Strip hotel and not on the west side of town.

I never did find out who conjured up this stupid idea to build on the west side. Many of the media folks felt the same way, but we broadcasters and writers had to refrain from criticizing the hotels. One false comment and your complimentary tickets and meals ('comps') were gone.

The way the boys generated money at Strip hotels, money spent on the Moulin Rogue was just a drop in the bucket. Nate Schlafer of the Sands ran the operation until its demise.

The Tournament of Champions, which features players who have won a PGA-sponsored tournament, started in the early '50's. The man who created this outstanding tournament was Howard Capps, the host pro at the Desert Inn Country Club, adjacent to the Desert Inn Hotel.

Before his stint at the D.I. Howard worked for Fred Waring at his course, Shawnee on the Delaware, in Pennsylvania.

The Desert Inn bigwigs, namely Wilbur Clark and Moe Dalitz and the rest of the reigning group, loved the venue because it brought the D.I. national recognition. It featured the best golf pros of that era. The tournament also attracted the high rollers who came to play and to watch the pro golfers in Tinseltown.

Gene Littler was a big winner by taking the title three consecutive years. In those days there was a Calcutta pool where golfers could place a bet on who they thought would win, and singer Frankie Laine (*That's My Desire*) was the big winner by picking Gene Littler the three years he won at the Desert Inn. Rumor had it that Laine's take was close to a half-million dollars. That was huge in those days.

The PGA (USGA) banned any Calcuttas when they got wind of what was taking place in Vegas. There is no such thing today.

The Tournament of Champions moved to La Costa in the San Diego area when Moe Dalitiz and the boys sold the Desert Inn to Howard Hughes. It has since moved to Hawaii and is played at the beginning of January each year. The format remains the same, with only tour winners participating.

Howard Capps departed Vegas and bought a nine-hole course in Napa, California. He was a great pro and loved by everyone. He was replaced at the Desert Inn Country Club by touring pro, Bo Winninger.

Julius Boros checking over his score card at the Tournament of Champions at the Desert Inn

Chuck Hull and Announcer-Engineer Gordon Attebury announce the golf tournament in Las Vegas for KLAV, the station I managed

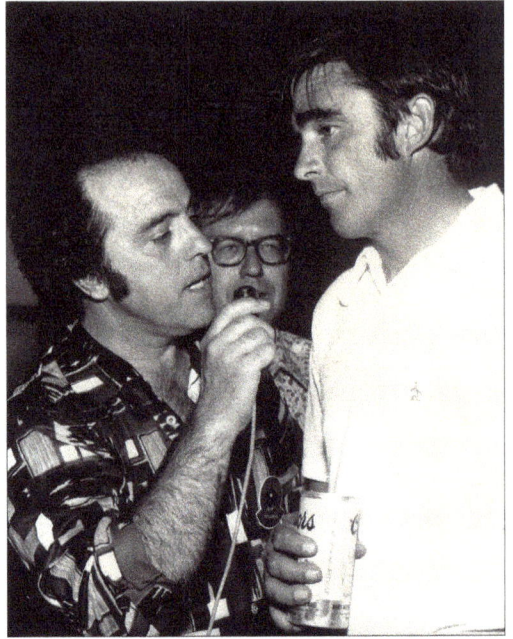

SELLING INSURANCE

There was a period in the late 50's where I felt that radio was a little boring and I decided (while still working in radio), to get into the insurance business.

I studied the various aspects of insurance with two other interested parties, and eventually, we took the state exam, passed it, and then I started selling insurance for the first time in my life. I was selling life, accident, and health insurance.

Well, to my surprise, compared to radio, it was not interesting, nor did I delight in it. Also, when friends saw me, they would run for cover because they felt I was going to pitch them to buy insurance. Further, in radio, there were more perks, and it was more creative…figuring out what tunes to play as a disc jockey for my daily show, and what star appearing on the Las Vegas Strip was I going to meet and interview.

It was a no-brainer for the decision I made, and that was to remain in radio, which I loved more than insurance. I probably would have become a rich man had I stayed in the insurance field because selling was no problem, but I have no regrets.

Many of my friends have carved their niche in insurance and I applaud them. But I think I made the right decision to remain a radio geek. My suggestion is to follow your heart in whatever endeavor you pursue.

It was great to live in Las Vegas in the '50's and '60's. Everyone was working in every facet of society and making good wages, whether they were dealers, waitresses, parking lot attendants, servers, or management personnel. Everyone was swingin' to the tune of the times. Most importantly, the locals made their wages in town and spent them locally. If they had to purchase an auto, they naturally went to the local dealers and not to Los Angeles to save a buck or two, as is the case where I live now.

One of the popular auto agencies in Sin City was the James Cashman Cadillac Co., a very aggressive car dealership with longevity in Clark County. The family was well respected and known throughout the desert area.

Besides the green folding money people made, silver coins were prevalent during those years, and change was given in that manner. The problem with silver dollars was that they were heavy, and after a time, a pocket would wear out of shape from the weight. Naturally, the practice of giving change in silver dollars went bust - to the delight of the recipient, but not for the tailors who were busy repairing holes in pockets.

Talk about hindsight. What if we had all the silver dollars from the years we spent in Vegas and cashed them in today? The weight factor wouldn't mean a thing. As the saying goes, "What did I know, and why should I? Brain surgery is my specialty!"

Who knew?

My mission was to be a top broadcaster.

PUBLIC RELATIONS PEOPLE

What do you think most generated Las Vegas' popularity? Who was responsible for its quick assent? I think it was a total pubic relations job put forth by a group of publicity directors who were without a doubt the best in the world. No expense was spared to promote Las Vegas through direct advertising in the major markets, along with wining and dining the top radio, TV personalities, and society writers, both locally and nationally.

The hotels and their publicity directors were as follows: Gene Murphy at Wilbur Clark's Desert Inn, Herb MacDonald at the Sahara Hotel, Hal Braudis at the Thunderbird Hotel, Maury Stevens at the Frontier Hotel, Lee Fisher and Jean Magowan at the Dunes Hotel, and Harvey Diederich at the Tropicana Hotel. Al Freeman at the Sands Hotel was the PR person I was closest to. He was always there for the first-time invites and made sure we were well supplied with recordings from those recording artists who appeared at their hotel.

"Killer Diller" Abe Schiller was another publicity person who extended himself over and above for the press during his years at the Flamingo Hotel. Abe wore western garb year round and he was known as the 'Jewish Cowboy.'

We mustn't forget Nick Naff, John Romero, and Dick Kanellis, all of whom worked at the Sahara Hotel from 1953 to 1968. Each did a commendable job promoting the hotel.

Since I departed Las Vegas, nothing has changed in that department, with bigger and better hotels appearing on the Strip and near environs. Also, sporting venues have added to the publicity of this fabulous city.

Every syndicate that had its claws in Vegas gambling had what was known as a bag man, whether the syndicate emanated from Miami, New Orleans, Cleveland, or another city.

The bag man had to be a trusted soul, because the boys wouldn't send someone to Vegas who wouldn't return with the cash in the amount they anticipated. Rumor had it that when the boys fronted the money to build or purchase a hotel, they were reimbursed on a monthly basis by one of their members coming to Las Vegas, and while there, visited the counting room where the monies were accumulated. Those in charge of the room knew the visitor, who had total access. Naturally, the visitor was a friend of the man in the counting room.

There was a joke about the bag man when I lived in Las Vegas. It went like this:

He counted two for me and one for Uncle Sam, etc. Now mind you, this bag man was very dapper and looked like your typical businessman. He filled his bag and went on his way, catching the first plane back to his city. When there, he turned it over to that fellow in charge, and the monies were distributed. Of course, if he thought he could pull a fast one and didn't return, his life was in imminent danger.

If this occurred today, which I'm sure it doesn't, they would have to take private flights to avoid having to go through security screen at commercial airports.

When the corporate men took over Las Vegas, the bag man was eliminated, as were the men who sent him there. Plus, just before I left Las Vegas, the IRS was beginning to make its move on all the hotels to make sure none of the boys still had a piece of the hotel action.

You can thank Del Webb and Howard Hughes for the change in Las Vegas gaming and making it a corporate operation, where all monies had to be accounted for. So the bag man became a thing of the past.

LOUNGE ENTERTAINMENT

In the early 50's, Stan Irwin and the bigwigs at the Sahara Hotel revolutionized entertainment on the Strip by starting lounge acts featuring new and exciting groups, two of which were the Mary Kaye Trio with Frankie Ross and Louis Prima, and Sam Butera and the Witnesses with vocalist Keely Smith.

Lounge groups brought a new innovation in entertainment, drawing tremendous crowds who either couldn't get into the main showroom, or just wanted to have a toddy and watch a great show. These groups were the precursor of hundreds of lounge shows, which followed the Sahara's lead. It was also a way to keep the gambling patron in the hotel after the main show in an auditorium (which seated two to four hundred people).

The Mary Kaye Trio started it all; they were also recording on the Decca label. Ross was the comic of the trio. Norman sang and was the straight man to sister Mary, who was the lead singer.

Following the popularity of the Mary Kaye Trio, the Sahara brought in Louis Prima and his crew directly from New Orleans, where Louis was born. Sam Butera played the honking tenor sax and sang. The group included singer Keely Smith, Lou Sino on trombone, Rollie Dee on bass, Morgan Thomas on trumpet, and Jimmy Vincent on drums.

Prima was a great trumpet player and quite a composer. He was responsible for penning *Sing, Sing, Sing* and *Sunday Kind Of Love*, both American standard tunes. Benny Goodman had the big hit on *Sing, Sing, Sing*.

Once the lounge acts became popular at the Sahara, all the other hotels got on the musical bandwagon. Today it's commonplace to see and hear groups and comedians in the various lounges.

So, when you visit Las Vegas and catch a lounge act, remember it all started in the early '50's and that credit goes to the Sahara Hotel for being the innovators.

During the filming of *Ocean's Eleven* in 1960, the Desert Inn was one of the shooting locales. In one of the scenes (the countdown to midnight), before the robbery took place in the movie (New Year's Eve), the announcer who was counting down the time was Robert Bock, my program director at KLAS in Las Vegas; he was a real talent, even though he was quite young.

Bob had a great radio voice and was chosen over other candidates to handle the New Year's Eve countdown. In one of the Las Vegas stories in our book, he's the one who is mentioned where a trick was played on the world-renowned announcer, Jean Paul King.

Most of the Rat Pack members had parts in the movie, and since the first *Ocean's Eleven* film, there have been two or three follow up movies, featuring George Clooney in the second rendition.

Getting back to Bock, he was paid a nice fee for his stint in the movie and became a member of SAG (Screen Actor's Guild). This also enhanced his resume when it came time to audition for the job at KRLA, one of the big radio stations in Los Angeles. Bob handled the news there and wasn't spinning records as he was at KLAS in Las Vegas.

Ocean's Eleven brought great notoriety to Las Vegas and was another feather in the city's publicity cap; the Strip survived on constant promotion, whether local or national. That was part of the make-up of Glitter Gulch. Promote it any way you can to entice people to come and spend money. Have fun in our town, but keep the green stuff coming.

When I mentioned to friends that I was contemplating writing a book on Las Vegas, the younger folks who read and heard about the Rat Pack were enthused. They wanted to know what took place during those exciting days and nights.

The Rat Pack consisted of Frank Sinatra, Dean Martin, Sammy Davis, Jr., Joey Bishop, and Peter Lawford. There are some pundits who add a few more characters, such as Angie Dickson and others, but the aforementioned and no one else were the Rat Pack. Naturally there were hangers-on, but that's normal with popular show people. In some cases they are what is known as 'groupies.' They ate and drank what the stars had to offer and supported them both emotionally and with their pocketbooks.

The Rat Pack appeared exclusively at the Sands Hotel where Jack Entratter, the GM, and his able and talented publicity director, Al Freeman, always had the top press people on hand for opening night. Rest assured, the highest rollers were in attendance with everything comped, from rooms to food.

Every member of the Rat Pack got in on the comedy routines and verbiage, and many of their stints were ad lib. But not the singing by Frank, Dean, and Sammy.

Many times after a show, the Rat Pack would make the rounds at other hotels and continue their shenanigans, much to the delight of the patrons and hotel owners.

Since the Rat Pack, there has never been another group to excite the Vegas patrons. It's an era never to be duplicated again.

Today, there are some groups who emulate the Rat Pack in looks and comedy who do a commendable job, but there was only one Rat Pack.

In today's world of interpretation one must watch one's P's and Q's. But the same was true in the '50's and '60's, so in that sense, nothing has changed.

When I first worked in fabulous Las Vegas, the mayor was Oran Gragson, someone I would call a regular person but not your mental giant! He was a respectable mayor but very simpatico. He wasn't one of the most dynamic of speakers, but he did keep the city percolating.

I remember once there was a little conflict on the west side of town where the majority of residents were black. Whatever the issue, because it was in that part of town, it made the news on television, radio, and in the newspapers.

Both TV stations (KORK and KLAS) had their reporters on the scene after an incident which wasn't a full blown riot, but there was enough noise and video to cause consternation and worry among Las Vegans.

Mayor Gragson made his appearance on the scene at a press conference to calm the nerves of those affected. That's what any good mayor would do. But this mayor held a question and answer session to accommodate the media. When one reporter asked the mayor what he was going to do about the problem on the west side, Mayor Gragson replied, "Well, when we get to the bottom of this, we're going to call a spade, a spade." There was silence in the room as the media waited for the mayor to realize what he'd said. But he didn't, he simply continued his press conference.

In today's world, he would have to face the music for his dumb statement, even though it was an innocent remark. When speaking to the masses, or to a small group, one must be careful not to offend anyone. Sometimes it's difficult to ad-lib!

JUICE JOBS

Juice jobs were the hardest jobs to come by, and it was imperative to have a friend who could get you in on the action. Many of the Juice Jobs were handed down from father to son, relative to relative, friend to friend; whether it was for maitre d', waiter, dealer, or culinary jobs. They were good jobs that were awarded based not on what you knew, but on who you knew; a good connection was juice. Parking lot attendants were also in the good job category.

The hotels were run by syndicates from Cleveland, Chicago, Miami, New York, etc. If you knew any of the main characters or were raised with them, then you were assured a good job at the hotel they ran.

It had been rumored, on good authority, that some of the maitre d's at Strip hotels were knocking down from a hundred to two hundred thousand dollars a year, and that was all cash. If you attended one of their shows and didn't want to sit behind a pillar, and had folding money in your hand, then you sat down at ringside. In Vegas, money talked, and you-know-what walked. Wallets were unheard of; everyone carried folding money, and they spent it willingly. There were no cheapskates in Sin City. Everyone made good money, and they spent accordingly.

Dealer positions went easily to those who dealt cards at card rooms in New Orleans, Stubenville, Ohio, and other areas where some type of gambling took place, and the applicant had connections through the bosses there.

So if you hear the term 'Juice Jobs,' you'll know what that person is talking about.

All the radio personalities in Las Vegas during the '50's and '60's were always called upon to be masters of ceremonies for many events, including sporting venues or some big social affairs. Remember, it was a period when Las Vegas was growing with more hotel openings and new shopping centers, along with new homes being built.

Those radio celebrities who were on constant call were Martin Black, Gus Giuffre, Hal Morelli, Chuck Hull, Dick Gregg, Len Howard, and this reporter.

Hotel public relations men were the first to call us, and we seldom turned them down. We were all on their VIP list, and they treated us royally, so it was a win-win situation. Seldom was any money involved for your services, and we didn't request, either. Incidentally, there was never any competition amongst announcers who worked for different radio stations or those who hosted television shows. In Las Vegas, the media was a great fraternity, and we all got along…it wasn't like today's dog-eat-dog competition. I liked it better in those days.

Golfers Attention!

THE TOURNAMENT OF CHAMPIONS

Brought to You LIVE, Direct From

THE 18TH GREEN

DESERT INN COURSE

5 TIMES A DAY

By Sam Salerno

APRIL 29, 30 MAY 1, 2

ON

RADIO'S QUALITY VOICE

"Kay Luck"

RADIO **KLUC**

1050 AM DIAL   98.5 FM DIAL

"CBS--Your News Address"

NAVY RELIEF SHOW PLANNED — Plans for the Lake Mead Navy Relief dinner-dance show are being made by Hal Morelli, seated right, prominent radio-TV personality; Bob Fowler, coordinator for the Base; seated, Howard Senor, PR director for the Hotel Flamingo; standing left and Sam Salerno. Morelli and Salerno, along with Gus Giuffre and Dick Gregg, are serving as Masters of Ceremonies for the event.

Martin Black was called upon to broadcast the first horse racing event, which was situated by the new Convention Center. For a guy who was a good broadcaster handling interviews and news stories, he didn't do a bad job. But he realized it wasn't his forte. Chuck Hull and I covered golf tournaments, and there was a time when the state basketball tournament was handled by this reporter.

There was always some event happening in Las Vegas, and one of the aforementioned announcers would get the call to be the M.C.!

RANCHO GRIDDER HONORED—Marsh Evans, Rancho High senior, receives a certificate from Sam Salerno of radio station KLAS acclaiming the Ram footballer for his selection to the Wigwam Wisemen's second All-America team.

Talk of the Town

— Dolores Spencer, Women's Editor —

6 Las Vegas Review-Journal   Friday, October 15, 1965

'We Heard'

Italian Dinner

Huge Success

By ANN VALDER
Assistant Women's Editor

The first Annual Columbus Day celebration by the Italian American Club of Southern Nevada and the Las Vegas Order, Sons of Italy in America was held in the Crown Jewel Room of the Dunes Hotel on Columbus Day and was a huge success with many notables attending: Gov. Grant Sawyer, Sen. Alan Bible, Sen. Howard Cannon, Cong. Walter S. Baring, Mayor Oran Gragson, Lt. Gov. Paul Laxalt, Judge David Zenoff, State Sen. Mahlon Brown, and Mrs. Jimmy Durante, who accepted the achievement award for her husband who was unable to attend; William Raggio and Bruno Giuffrida.

Seen at the gala affair were Mr. and Mrs. Mike Mirabelli, "Pop" and Mrs. M. Mirabelli, Judge and Mrs. William Compton, Jeanne Drew, Mrs. Sidney Whitmore, Nick Keliv, Sheriff and Mrs. Ralph Lamb, District Attorney and Mrs. Edward G. Marshall, the Joe Rue's, Eileen Brookman, Don Giuffridas, Angelo Manzis, Harry Levys, Donald Gildays, Pete Bommaritos, Carl Eggers, Nick Varas, Clem Poechmanns and their son Richard, JoAnn Carr and the Frankie Carrs.

Gus Giuffre, Sam Salerno and Hal Morelli were master of ceremonies.

NEWS

FROM
Hotel Tropicana News Bureau,
LAS VEGAS, NEVADA
Telephone: 736-4949

FOR IMMEDIATE RELEASE

May 27, 1968

In cooperation with Musician's Union, Local 369, the Hotel Tropicana is continuing a series of jazz concerts featuring the finest Las Vegas musicians.

Tommy Vig and his group will be spotlighted in the hotel's Blue Room early Sunday morning from 3 to 4 a.m.

Trumpeters Don Ellis and Red Rodney will be united for the first time. Other artists on the bandstand include Gus Mancuso, Carl Saunders and Ernie McDaniel.

Sam Salerno, local radio personality, will act as master of ceremonies for the Vig concert.

-30-

LAS VEGAS HIGH SCHOOL

QUARTERBACK CLUB, INC.

4224 DOVER PLACE
DU 2-1900

1958-59
PRESIDENT
MARTIN DALY
VICE PRESIDENT
DOD HOST
SECRETARY & TREASURER
BRUCE TRENT
DIRECTORS
CURTIS TRAHAN
HANS WALDMAN
DR. A. H. LOVAAS
FLETCHER WELLINGTON

August 11, 1958

Sam Salerno
KLAS Radio
Los Angeles Highway
Las Vegas, Nevada

Dear Sam:

The Las Vegas Quarterback Club is looking ahead to an outstanding 1958 football season.

On Wednesday morning, August 20th, we are holding our football kick-off Quarterback Club breakfast (time and place to be announced). Our guest speaker will be Elroy (Crazy Legs) Hirsch. We would like to invite you to attend this affair as the guest of our club and be an active member in all of our 1958 seasons functions.

Enclosed you will find your paid-up Membership Card. Please join with us to help make this season the best yet.

Sincerely,

H. B. Trent

H. B. Trent, Secretary
Quarterback Club

HBT/wd

Enc.

"A BOOSTER CLUB DEDICATED TO THE BOYS & GOOD SPORTSMANSHIP"

I'M A TENOR - NOT A BARITONE

This incident occurred during my deejay stint in Las Vegas on KLAV. My show featured the top recording artists of the day(Sinatra, Goulet, Clooney, etc.), and interviews with those stars appearing at Strip hotels. All interviews were set up by the publicity directors of each hotel. Some were live; others were pre-recorded for later broadcast.

Sergio Franchi was the featured star at the Sahara Hotel, and I made arrangements to get an interview with him. At the time, he was hot on records, TV, and public appearances.

The interview was not live but recorded and played on my show at a designated time. The show aired from 6 to 9 a.m., Monday through Friday.

I went to his hotel room for the interview and was greeted warmly by Mr. Franchi.

Having studied voice and been around music all my life and cognizant of sound, I was under the illusion that Mr. Franchi was a baritone because of the strength of his voice and its tonal quality.

I started the tape recording at a designated time and the interview began as follows:

"And now, appearing at the Sahara Hotel, the star of the show, baritone Sergio Franchi!"

Well, Sergio hit the ceiling and said, "Io sono tenora!" He was not a baritone, he was a tenor, and red-faced, I stopped the machine, rolled the tape back, and (blushingly) started over.

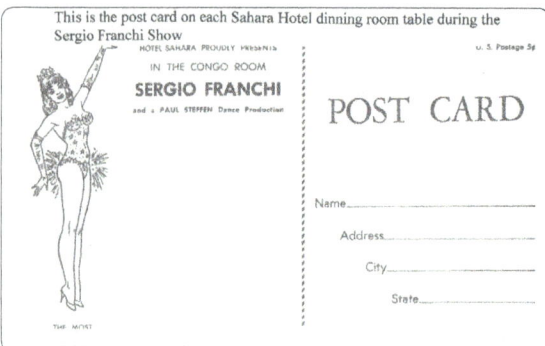

This is the post card on each Sahara Hotel dinning room table during the Sergio Franchi Show

HOTEL SAHARA PROUDLY PRESENTS
IN THE CONGO ROOM
SERGIO FRANCHI
and a PAUL STEFFEN Dance Production

POST CARD

U. S. Postage 3¢

Name_____

Address_____

City_____

State_____

THE MOST

Perhaps I should have done my homework better and not relied on a tone that resounded in my head and gave me the impression Mr. Franchi was a baritone. Red faced, I paid my respects and said good bye.

Wonder what Sergio thought...

THE JERSEY BOYS

When I was managing radio station KLAV in Las Vegas, I wasn't your typical executive who sits behind a desk and dictates orders. I was a hands-on manager and spent most of my time on the street soliciting ads for the station.

There was a new business opening up on Main Street called Imperial Carpet Company, and the owners were from New Jersey. Paul Wolfson was one owner and Julie Laikin was the other. They were equal partners, and each excelled in all facets of the carpet business. They came to town as pros in the carpet field.

When I met them, they were laying the carpet for their own building, which really impressed me. I was there to help them to exploit their product through radio spots, mainly through a personal touch on my morning radio show.

Well, our friendship lasted as long as I was working in Las Vegas. We also socialized a good deal by attending many show openings on the Las Vegas Strip. Because of their expertise in their chosen profession, Paul and Julie made friends with the right hotel operators, and their business flourished. At first, they laid the carpet, but eventually they had a crew to handle that part of the operation.

Wolfson lived in the west part of town, an area where I resided when I married my accountant wife.

When Julie died, his share of the business went to his son, Herb, who was just as sharp as his dad. He was still at Imperial Carpet when I left to purchase KRML in Carmel.

The Jersey Boys proved that with hard work and the right attitude, one can make it anywhere, even in Las Vegas!

The media wasn't as powerful in the early days as it is today with smartphones, tweeting, etc., but the written word was powerful and could literally break a person.

The *Las Vegas Sun* and the *Las Vegas Review Journal* were the two newspapers that locals read. Both had good reporters and columnists whose columns were read regularly. The *Sun* had Ralph Pearl and Murray Hertz, and the *Review Journal* had Forrest Duke. *The Review Journal* (Don Ray Media), also owned KORK-TV and KORK Radio. Hank Greenspun later purchased KLAS-TV. Howard Hughes later bought the CBS affiliate from Greenspun.

One writer whose pen could destroy a person or a politician was Hank Greenspun, owner and editor of the *Las Vegas Sun*. Everyone in town read his column, "Where I Stand," and if Hank didn't like what a certain politician was doing, he would blast him in his column. He very seldom picked on the hotels, because they all advertised in his newspaper. Hank also had repartee with many honchos running the hotels, so it would behoove him to go easy on them!

Greenspun was quite powerful through his column. One particular person who drew his ire was Bill Peccole, a politician and, if memory serves me, a councilman whose histrionics did not conform to Greenspun's philosophy. Hank constantly pounded him in his book *Where I Stand*, which he wrote with Alex Pelle, and eventually Bill Peccole was seldom heard from and was a defeated man.

In addition to his newspaper holding, Greenspun was a big property owner and was doing well with his newspaper and television station. If you were his friend and your philosophies were the same, everything was kosher. If you crossed him or did something he thought was negative to the city's progress, run for cover. Hank was tough but fair and helped in Las Vegas's growth.

THE MORMON INFLUENCE

Las Vegas was a railroad stop long before it became a gambling mecca. There were some card rooms and slot machines downtown at the Boulder Club, the Las Vegas Club, and Golden Nugget.

The Mormons were part of the populace in Nevada and likewise in the contiguous states of Arizona and Utah; hard working people and kind of oblivious to gambling, which was not in their DNA and was prohibited in their religion, as was the drinking of coffee and alcoholic beverages.

It took those of Italian extraction and those of the Jewish faith to awaken the Mormons on how to make money - and lots of it! When they realized what was happening in Glitter Gulch, they immediately jumped on the money bandwagon. There were no edicts in the Mormon religion against purchasing property on or near the Strip. They were not against progress, their own or that of the community. Some of the top lawyers, doctors, and other professional people were of the Mormon faith, and their input was essential to the growth of Las Vegas. They became part of the city's growth.

Many Mormons owned pristine property on the Strip and other properties the casino owners were interested in; thus grew the Mormon influence in the gaming industry. Mormons became politicians, and the hotel owners needed their influence in many of their projects related to new hotels, roads, etc.

Playing golf at the Las Vegas Municipal Golf Course in Las Vegas was a means of improving my game and meeting some interesting locals.

I became acquainted with a player who turned out to be the former lead singer for Fred Waring and the Pennsylvanians. He had retired from professional singing and was now part of the Las Vegas fabric.

His name was Joe Marine, a nice looking fellow who was well-mannered. We hit it off as friends and became regulars with a couple of other golfers, and Saturday was the day we tore up some turf at the locals' favorite course. The price was right, and most of the golf hacks played there. None of us was what you would consider a serious golfer. Joe was the longest hitter in our group, and at times he could reach the five-pars in two, which gave him a chance for an eagle putt.

I had Joe on my radio show more than once, and invariably we played *Birth of the Blues*, which was featured on a two-record set by Fred Waring. (In another chapter of this book I mention Howard Capps, the pro at the Desert Inn, and the fact that he worked at Waring's golf course at Shawnee on the Delaware.)

No longer singing professionally, Joe worked for McKesson Liquors, a large distributing firm which supplied most of the Las Vegas Strip hotels with their liquor. He became one of their top salesmen during his stint there.

Meeting people like Joe Marine in Las Vegas was not uncommon in the early Vegas days. Every professional wanted to go there because of all the job opportunities, and because the money was good. Joe was my first guest on the new show, *Dining at The Alpine Village Inn*, located on the Las Vegas Strip.

Great German food!

Joe Marine, former top vocalist for Fred Waring, is my guest at the Alpine Village on the Strip.

I was comfortable handling a morning show on radio as opposed to working a late shift, for I felt my voice had better resonance in the early hours, and I was more alert to give the time, play what I felt listeners wanted to hear, and read the news from the wire machine more easily. I hope my listeners felt the same.

Rube Jolley, a Mormon, was the owner of KLAS at the time, and when he wasn't running the radio station, he was playing golf at the Desert Inn Country Club. He treated me well, particularly when I had my tonsils taken out and was laid up for some six months. I was working, but my voice just wasn't right for a good spell. Rube didn't lose faith in me and had me work in another capacity, other than announcing.

We had three top disc jockeys at the time, yours truly handling *Coffee Time* from the hours of 8:10 to 10 a.m., with Bob Bock following me, and after his stint it was Lowell Cannon filling the airwaves with great sounds in the evening hours. Interspersed with the music was our coverage from CBS News which was heard on the hour straight up.

When we weren't on the air, Cannon and I were out trying to garner some radio ads to help the station from a commercial standpoint. KLAS was smart enough to run print ads in the *Las Vegas Sun*. The *Las Vegas Review Journal* was owned by the Don Rae Media Group, which owned the NBC television station in the market.

Our newspaper ad read, "CBS, for Cannon, Bock, and Salerno." All these promo ads were sent to CBS to show how our station promoted their product.

INTERVIEWS FOR ITALIAN LISTENING — Erberto Landi, free-lance announcer for Voice or America in Italy, is pictured with Sam Salerno, right, of radio station KLAV. Landi is preparing a series of interviews with strip performers for beaming throughout Italy.

— REVIEW-JOURNAL PHOTO

Strip Performers Tape Recorded for Voice of America Broadcasts in Italy

4 Las Vegas Review-Journal   Wednesday, Mar. 6, 1968

Local Broadcasters Elect Ed Tabor as New President

The Southern Nevada Broadcasters Association, a group of radio and television executives operating area stations, elected new officers Tuesday.

The president is Ed Tabor, vice president and general manager of KORK—TV; vice president is Sam Salerno, manager of KLAV radio; secretary is Mark Smith, manager of KLAS—TV, and treasurer is Bat Henderson, manager of KVEG radio.

To serve for one year, the officers were selected at a regular meeting at the Flamingo Hotel.

Part of the popularity of Las Vegas was gained from radio broadcasts that were heard on the *Voice of America,* which was available in most countries and particularly in Italy, mainly because of the efforts of Erberto Landi, who came to Las Vegas to record shows to be aired abroad with this voice.

At the time, I was program director of KLAS, the CBS affiliate, located on the grounds of the Desert Inn Hotel.

Erberto's job was to get interviews with the Vegas Strip personalities. He was an attorney and also a member of the press, so he had knowledge of the media. Not knowing enough about Las Vegas, he called on me to help him get the interviews because of my contacts with the hotel public relations men.

He and I got along, and on occasion we spoke a few words in Italian - not the King's English Italian from my part, because I was never schooled properly in that language - but I could manage a conversation.

Along with all his other talents, Landi was instrumental in booking quite a few Italian artists in the United States, so he was kind of a jack of all trades, using everything he learned and then applying it to broadcasting, journalism, and legal matters.

Before World War II, he was an announcer for Italian language radio stations. He was also was employed by the Office of War Information, a part of NBC's national division.

The broadcasts further helped me establish a greater relationship with most of Strip hotel public relation folks. Another feather in my cap!

Marquee stature was most important to entertainers, and they were very particular how large the letters were on their names at the hotels' billboards. They were adamant about who really was the star of a given show at a Strip hotel. A lesser known star couldn't supersede or have larger letters on the marquee.

Hotel owners and public relations moguls couldn't mess with a star's ego. I guess it was, and still is, a part of a star's persona. It hasn't changed and never will, regardless of the era.

Would you believe that at one time I glanced up at the Riviera Hotel marquee, and star billing went to Liberace, the flamboyant pianist, and at times, singer. Guess who was second billed? Well, it was singer Barbra Streisand. She was just becoming known through her recordings and personal appearances. After her rise to stardom, Barbra became the main attraction at all venues and received top billing on the marquee.

On the other side of the Strip, at the Old Frontier Hotel, I glanced at the marquee, and the headliner was Freddy Martin and his orchestra, which featured singer (later to become a big star) Merv Griffin. Second billing on this marquee was Elvis Presley. Yes, I said Elvis Presley. He, too, was just beginning in show business.

Two surprises taking place in the early heyday of Las Vegas. That all changed with Barbra and Elvis becoming mega stars, but, like all entertainers, this was their beginning. It was an exciting time in early Las Vegas.

VIP LIST

Las Vegas hotel public relations men were the very best in the business and knew how to promote a show or an event. They spared no expense to get the word out to the general public via radio, television, and newspapers. This was the norm for them, regardless of what they were promoting. This could mean their show, exploiting a new entertainer, or giving information about a new restaurant, or a sporting event the hotel was involved in.

The VIP list consisted of the top television and radio personalities, and the top columnist for the *Las Vegas Sun* or the *Las Vegas Review Journal*. If you were on the hotel's list, then you would receive a phone invite or a telegram for a specific show; there were neither e-mails nor faxes in those days.

For the radio jocks, there were just a few privy to this type of invite. During the early 50's it was Hal Morelli, Gus Guiffre, Martin Black, Barney Sullivan, Joe Julian, Jack Kogan, Jim Hart, Ralph Pearl, Joe Delaney, Murray Hertz, and yours truly, who hosted *Sam The Morning Man* from 6 to 9 a.m., interviewing Strip entertainers, comics, and singers.

At these shows, everything was complimentary, including food and drinks. At times, gifts were included.

This is how the word got out to the nation, and, by virtue of this exploitation, tourism started to flourish, and the high rollers made their way to Glitter Gulch.

Besides the Visitors and Convention Bureau, each hotel had its own group soliciting conventions. Again, it was a total promotional package extended by the hotels. There were a number of locals who traveled to cities around the country tossing about silver dollars to entice club groups to meet in Las Vegas.

Want a PR lesson? Then take a trip to Las Vegas to see how it's done.

Lowell Cannon and me, covering the action at a Vegas golf tournament

The sports "broadcast crew" from KLAV. Ernie Russell, me, Chuck Hull, and Gordon Attebery...a versatile group

COVERING SPORTS IN LAS VEGAS

As a program director or a radio station manager, it was imperative in the early radio days in Las Vegas to conjure up new ideas to increase the station's revenues, rather than just sell radio spots.

Las Vegas was a hip sports city, and just about anyone connected with the gaming industry was a sports fan, interested in baseball, football, and golf. So if a sporting event took place that struck one's fancy in Glitter Gulch, we at KLAV made sure we covered the event, selling the entire package or adjacent spots sandwiched between the venue.

It was an easy sell to the Strip hotels, or those casinos in downtown Las Vegas. We covered the Tournament of Champions golfing event, the Sahara Invitational Tournament, and the Stardust Tournament (for the LPGA). There was always an interest from the station's point of view, and also from those who sponsored the event. Most of those big shots connected to hotels were sports enthusiasts.

There was no secret in the motive of our coverage of these events, because we were well prepared with an announcing crew second to none. The group included Chuck Hull, who later became the TV host for all boxing venues emanating from the city. Ernie Russell, a free-lance sportscaster and this writer, loved covering sporting events. Lowell Cannon, who co-managed KLAV with me for a short period, also handled the mic chores during golf coverage at KLAV.

I must admit, other stations were on the scene, but none put in the effort or personnel as we did to achieve optimum results. We knew all the efforts would help the station's image and increase our dollar gross. It was all about the bottom line. Gordon Attebury was our chief engineer, and he was the best in town. All these facets made the reports the best in the Las Vegas area.

FOUR MILE BROTHEL: A WAY TO RELIEVE TENSION

When I arrived in Las Vegas in the early '50's, prostitution was legal as long as Glenn Jones was the sheriff.

The brothel was located four miles out of town on the Boulder Highway. If your testosterone levels were high and you wanted some relief, you made your way to Four Mile.

When you arrived there by auto you were greeted by three or four well-dressed men who looked like NFL football players. They showed you to the front door, where you entered and found a bevy of beautiful women. You made your selection and were accommodated during a 15-minute period. Mind you, when the bell rang you were through. If you did not reach you're goal (orgasm), too bad! Can you imagine that?

When Ralph Lamb became the new sheriff of Clark County, Four Mile was abolished. Having left Las Vegas in the latter part of 1968, I don't know if there are any brothels in Sin City today. Rumor has it that if you are a high roller today, the hotels can accommodate your sexual desires.

It's not that difficult to compare Las Vegas in the '50's and '60's and the Vegas of today. The difference? Today, it's a sprawling community with almost two million inhabitants in the metro area. With this kind of expansion come problems; more hotels, more employees, and more of everything. Youngsters on the Strip soliciting prostitutes with pictures of same for your perusal. There are hotels, more golf courses, more restaurants, more crime, and less control than in the past.

In the early days the hotel operators controlled everything, moreso than the local police. There were very few disturbances to put a crimp in the gambling. If there was a fight in the hotel, the participants were escorted to the outskirts of town and told never to return. If they did return, their fate was brutal - often death. There are many bodies buried in the sands of Clark County.

Nothing could disturb gambling, no one person or any incident which could cause distraction for the players. The boys knew how to run a business.

Another interesting component of Vegas gambling was that the casinos were the ones who had to make a profit; it wasn't the restaurants or the rooms. This all changed when Del Webb purchased the Sahara Hotel and Howard Hughes came to town and starting purchasing hotels and other properties. As was typical with corporate owners, every department had to show a profit. And that's the way it is today.

Personally, I liked the way it was when the BOYS ran Las Vegas.

24 LAS VEGAS SUN   Friday, May 8, 1959

SUN dial

By TAB TABET

IT WAS AN ENTHUSIASTIC Bill Miller who walked into the New Frontier Hotel Wednesday morning, fresh from his trip to Tokyo. Bill had only glowing reports of the Far East and its beautiful women, excellent food and modern architecture. Bill went to Japan a few weeks ago to view a Nipponese show called "Tokyo Showtime." He planned to bring it back to the Venus Room, if it met with his approval. Miller liked the 36-gal show, which includes some nudes, and sez he'll have it ready for the Venus Room by July 1. He also plans to redecorate the room and use a Japanese theme, including the serving of Japanese food and the wearing of Japanese costumes by waitresses.

ON THE SUNNY SIDE: Capable Sammy Mandelbaum, formerly a Riviera and Dunes captain, becomes a Flamingo lounge captain. . . . They're still talking about Susan Woods' costume in the new Minsky show. . . . Jeannie Paradine leaves the Dunes show to plan her forthcoming marriage. . . . Vic Damone sang and five girls cried. . . . The mail department of First Western Savings is running over with males since luscious Sue Burnett, from Tallahassee, Alabama, joined the FW family. . . . Panorama Market manager Art Turk is up and around after a serious operation. . . . The Foxy spot on KLAS Radio is a gasser. The gentlemen responsible for the Edward R. Murrow and Kitzel bit are Bob Bock and Sam Salerno—very big time. . . . Sy Schwartz of Schwartz Bros. men's store, leaves today with his wife Diane for a brief vacation at the Bahia in San Diego. . . .

Foxy's Deli was one of the hot spots for Jewish clientele and others in Vegas' heyday. Strip celebrities were often seen there day and night. Foxy's was located next to the Sahara Hotel on Las Vegas Boulevard. Abe Fox, the proprietor, was one helluva person, loved by Jews and gentiles alike. He and I became good friends; he was responsible for introducing me to my second wife, Dee Park, who was his accountant working for the CPA firm Engel & Engel. Abe was an advertiser with our radio station, or any radio station that I was associated with.

I recorded many commercials using various voices. One in particular was a commercial imitating Kitzel, the Jewish character on the Jack Benny Show. The Jewish dialect I used was right on and similar to the real person.

During a visit to Las Vegas, Kitzel's attorney heard the commercials and notified his client. They threatened to sue if Abe Fox did not remove his commercial from the radio station. We capitulated because neither Abe nor I nor the radio station needed to fight a lawsuit, one we would lose.

Six months later the gentleman who was known as Kitzel passed away, and we were again able to air that funny commercial. Both Abe and I breathed a sigh of relief.

During my radio stint in Las Vegas, I tried to play golf when the occasion presented itself, though it was something of a challenge, being a newlywed with three young children. The golf I played was at the Las Vegas Municipal Course, where John Difloure was the head pro and Jerry Belt the teaching pro.

I had played nine holes and was headed for the tenth tee; the nines were split from one area to another. As I approached the tee, an elderly gentleman asked if he could join me on the back nine. I agreed, and we went on our way. We chatted, and it turned out that he had heard of me on the air, and I recognized his name. He was John "Cliff" Friend, one of the most prolific song writers in America. Well, the meeting turned out to be one of the best relationships I've had in my entire life. We communicated regularly, and he sent me all the records performed by artists playing or singing his compositions.

Cliff wrote many of the Roaring Twenties tunes which were penned in the late '20's and '30's. He wrote at least 28 standard tunes and also wrote many for Broadway shows. Some of the tunes were *Freddy The Freshman*, and *Old Man Time*, recorded by Jimmy Durante and Phil Harris. Cliff was one of the top members of ASCAP and other publishing firms.

Cliff had some poignant words for me when I was going through a divorce. Later, when I worked for Louis Prima, Cliff gave me the sheet music of one of his songs to see if Louis would record his composition. He had gone to their office in Hollywood and made his pitch, and Keely's brother did everything but toss him on his behind. It was only natural that when I went to work for Louis in Las Vegas years later, Cliff approached me to see if Prima would consider recording the tune. It was called, Come *Over to My House, I Have A Big Surprise For You*, a double-entendre song. Prima never recorded Cliff's song

I never heard from Cliff after I left Sin City in 1968. His legacy lives on with all the music he wrote.

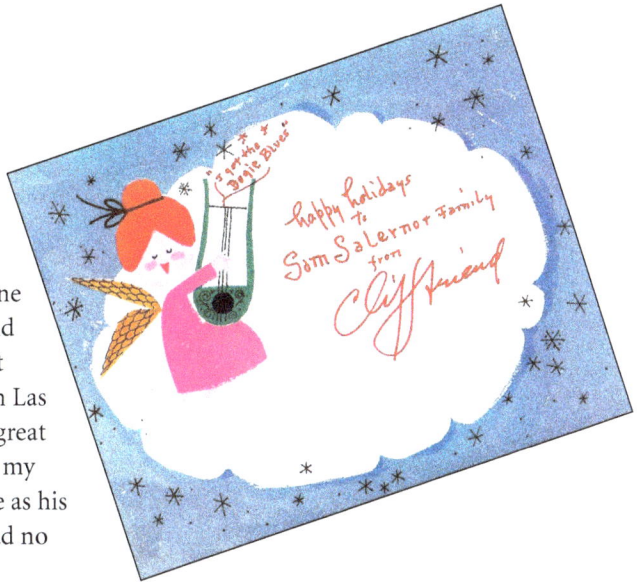

John "Cliff" Friend was one of the most interesting and talented people I ever met during the years I spent in Las Vegas. Not only was he a great person and talent, he was my mentor and he treated me as his surrogate son, since he had no children.

He related this true story to me that took place during the reign of Pancho Villa. He and his musical group were appearing in a nightclub in a border town close to Mexico, but in the United States.

Cliff was playing the piano and singing when the Mexican revolutionary general arrived with his entourage. He was escorting a black woman, perhaps his date, though Cliff couldn't recall. Cliff was vocalizing a tune and the word 'nigger' was part of the lyrics. (Remember, this goes back a century, a different time.) Well, when the black woman, who was sitting on Villa's lap, heard the lyrics and that word, she whispered something in his ear and it looked ominous for Cliff and his group. They stopped the music and headed for windows and doors, but Cliff was nabbed by Villa's men and taken outside for execution. The musicians all disappeared and Cliff was there to face his fate.

Well, Cliff pleaded that it was just a song and didn't reflect his feelings for black people. He stood before the firing squad, but Pancho's men never pulled the trigger. Somehow Pancho and his men believed Cliff's story about his not having written the lyrics; nor was he a 'racist,' as we would call him today.

Cliff was released by Pancho Villa, and the men went on their merry way. Here's maybe the most amazing part of this story: I asked Cliff whatever happened to his musician friends, and Cliff replied, "I haven't seen them to this day."

Part of my stint with KRAM, first located at the Flamingo Hotel (back by the pool area), and later located at the Riviera Hotel after Benny Gofstein and Gus Greenbaum sold the Flamingo Hotel and purchased the Riviera, was to interview recording stars and film bigwigs appearing at various Strip hotels. My show was called *Sam The Morning Man* and was heard from 6 to 9 a.m.

Ella Fitzgerald, the 'First Lady of Song' as she was called, was scheduled to appear on my show. Some of my jock radio friends warned me that Ella would be difficult to interview; that is, she would give direct 'yes' and 'no' answers to questions; she would not elaborate on her answers. This could prove to be a problem, because I enjoyed talking with those who were chatty and filled the desired air time. How could I cure Ella's ills? Well, I took a negative and made it a positive.

I pre-announced that Ella was going to be on the show and started the interview (prior to playing one of her recordings) with, "Ella, I've heard that you are hard to interview!" To which she replied, "Who told you that?" I said, "A little bird!" She quipped, "Well, you tell that little bird he's wrong!" And from then on, the interview went smoothly. We had a great get-together in words, and, naturally, playing her songs for an attentive audience. From that day on, Ella and I became good friends. During her stay at the hotel, I also borrowed a record player so she could listen to music during the daytime hours.

Ella & Duke at The Côte D'Azur

Verve

To Sam
The A.M. Man
all the best always

Ella Fitzgerald

Ella signs her album for me....what a person!

As you know later in life, Ella became a diabetic and lost both legs due to the ailment.

No one has come along since to duplicate her sound and lyric interpretations. Truly, she was The First Lady of Song!

The year was 1962, and the Tournament of Champions was the talk of the golf world because of its popularity and its unique format. Players could only participate if they won a sponsored PGA event. The tournament brought the best golfers and a host of celebrities who came to mingle with the touring pros, and to catch the great shows on the Las Vegas Strip.

"Seriously, though, I get a big kick out of playing golf here It's not every day that I get a chance to play in Crosby's back yard."

Golf Magazine was smart enough to do a great story (in color) about all the stars and celebs who played golf and who patronized the Vegas hotels. During their visit to the Desert Inn I had an opportunity to interview Bob Hope for part of the magazine story. What a thrill for this novice announcer; plus I got my puss in the national magazine.

The story told about the celebrities who played golf, including Natalie Wood and Bob Wagner, Tony Martin, Dagmar, Phil Harris, Walter Winchell, and Bing Crosby. The Desert Inn bosses, Allard Roen and Wilbur Clark, were also shown in the photos. Ray Bolger also made an appearance at the pro-celeb event, doing his usual shenanigans to generate some laughter. Crosby was probably the best golfer of the group, at one time carrying a single-digit handicap.

Richard Long and his wife Mara Corday also swatted a few balls to entice those who attended the event. Other celebrities who had their hand in golf at the time were Ida Lupino, John Wayne, Mexican actor Pedro Armendariz, Bob Newhart, Paulette Goddard, Jack Benny, and Al Jolson, who was an avid golfer.

I guess golf was the tonic for all the aforementioned stars to help them come back to the real world after performing. I know that there are many more stars and entertainers who love the game of golf.

Incidentally, Bob Hope presented me with a money clip and a set of cuff links depicting the famous Hope nose.

It was great to work in Las Vegas and to meet all the stars of Hollywood!

CBS RADIO

A Division of Columbia Broadcasting System, Inc.

485 MADISON AVENUE, NEW YORK 22, NEW YORK · PLAZA 1-2345

August 20, 1959

Mr. Sam Salerno
Radio Station KLAS
Box 1510
Wilbur Clark's Desert Inn
Las Vegas, Nevada

Dear Mr. Salerno:

Attached is a standard AFTRA agreement covering
your announcing of three MITCH MILLER programs.

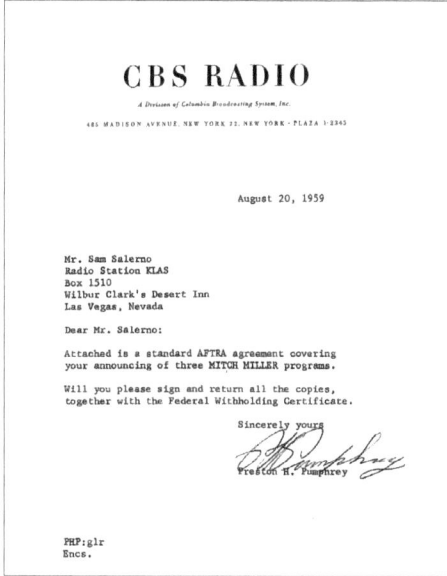

Will you please sign and return all the copies,
together with the Federal Withholding Certificate.

Sincerely yours,

Preston H. Pumphrey

PHP:glr
Encs.

The canceled check for my announcing gig at the Sands Hotel

While I was managing KLAS in Las Vegas I received a call from CBS Radio in New York that Mitch Miller, who hosted a weekly musical show on the network, was coming to the Sands Hotel to do a few interviews with celebrities to feature on his broadcast. I was not a regular member of AFTRA, but they gave me a temporary card so that I could handle the announcing chores for Mitch and his group.

The main attraction for the show featured the McGuire Sisters, who were appearing in Las Vegas and were a hot musical group at the time with many hit records. The McGuires also made headlines because of their associations with some sleazy characters. But their music on record was hard to beat, and they were in constant demand for their talent.

I was also happy for the gig because it meant extra cash for an announcer and station manager who wasn't making a large income. That was true of all media members in the '50's and '60's. Unless you were a network announcer (in the union), salaries were meager, but with most artists, we worked for the love of the profession.

For an intro, a radio spot at the half-way mark through the show, and a closing, I received $196.80, and after taxes, $166.19. Remember, that was in August of 1959.

Mitch Miller was great to work with, as were the McGuire Sisters, who were very friendly and accommodating. It was also a feather in the cap of my resume. There was an announcer in Los Angeles who was quite put out because the union gave me a temporary AFTRA card so I could handle the broadcast. He wanted to spend some leisure time in Las Vegas and pick up extra cash. C'est la vie!

The Crystal Room, America's Smartest Supper Club

DESERT INN PROUDLY PRESENTS

The McGUIRE SISTERS

TONY RIPOSO, MUSICAL CONDUCTOR

Material Written and Staged by
MURRAY KANE

GUY MARKS

Arirang Korean Revue

CARLTON HAYES
and his ORCHESTRA

SHOW TIMES
8:00 P.M. and
12 Midnight

CBS RADIO
A DIVISION OF COLUMBIA BROADCASTING SYSTEM, INC.

STANDARD AFTRA ENGAGEMENT CONTRACT FOR SINGLE RADIO
BROADCAST AND FOR MULTIPLE RADIO BROADCASTS
WITHIN ONE CALENDAR WEEK

Between
Dated: August 20, 1959

SAM SALERNO
Radio Station KLAS
Box 1510
Wilbur Clark's Desert Inn
Las Vegas, Nevada
(hereinafter called "Performer")

and

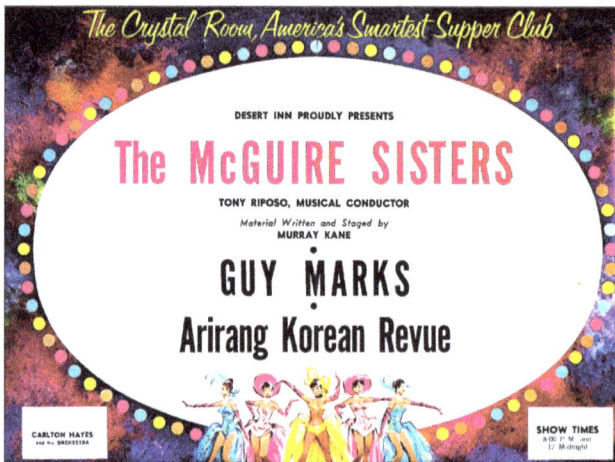

CBS RADIO, a Division of Columbia Broadcasting System, Inc.,
485 Madison Avenue, New York 22, New York
(hereinafter called "Producer").

Performer shall render artistic services in connection with the rehearsal and broadcast of the program(s) designated below and preparation in connection with the part or parts to be played:

TITLE OF PROGRAM: MITCH MILLER SHOW
TYPE OF PROGRAM: Local ( )   Network (x)   Sustaining (x)   Commercial (x)
SPONSOR(S) (if commercial):
DATE(S) AND TIME(S) OF PERFORMANCE:* Aug. 16, 23 and 30, 1959. 7:10-7:50 p.m. CHYT
PLACE OF PERFORMANCE: Las Vegas, Nevada
AFTRA CLASSIFICATION: Announcer
PART(S) TO BE PLAYED:
COMPENSATION: $65.60 per, or a total of $196.80
REHEARSALS:*
Date   From   To   Place   Date   From   To   Place

Execution of this agreement signifies acceptance by Producer and Performer of all the above terms and conditions and those on the reverse hereof and attached hereto, if any.

CBS RADIO, a Division of Columbia Broadcasting System, Inc.

Sam Salerno
Performer

By *[signature]*

DUDLEY 2-4070
Telephone Number

197-12-3443
Social Security Number

*Subject to change in accordance with AFTRA Code
F. CR 176-1/97

Form I had to sign to announce the Mitch Miller Show from the Sands Hotel

---

11/2/66

Forrest Duke

"The Visiting Fireman"

St. Jude Benefit Show
To Be One of Biggest

On Nov. 15 at the Riviera convention hall a benefit show for the St. Jude Ranch for homeless children (to be built in Boulder City) will be held, and it's rapidly shaping up as one of the biggest & best ever set for The Best City Of Them All.

Eddie Fisher, Jack Benny, Connie Francis, and Shecky Greene have accepted invitations to appear at the two-hour event. The Sheck will act as master of ceremonies, and many other stars, including Frank Sinatra, Joe E. Lewis, Trini Lopez, Dave Barry, George Shearing, Jackie Gayle, Shani Wallis, and The Treniers will also be invited to attend.

Mrs. Milton Prell and Norman B. Jonson have agreed to co-chairman the extravaganza, and the Trust Fund of Local 369, Musicians Union, is supplying the 13-piece orchestra under the direction of Lewis Elias. Food and beverages will come from the Riviera; in a later item more credits will be listed.

In the meantime, circle the date on your calendar, and Father Jack Adam, who is coordinating the fund-raiser (and is the man who conceived the wonderful idea of the St. Jude Ranch) will thank you in advance for your participation.

★   ★   ★

FRANK SINATRA, Leo Durocher, Bo Wininger, and Pat Henry joined Joe E. Lewis at his late (2:15) show Monday night at the Aladdin—what a laugh-riot THAT was! . . .

PHIL CROSBY was here for the Caesars Palace Halloween Costume Ball; he and DI doll Georgi Edwards (the former "Miss New Mexico") were in the "Hell's Angels" group which won a prize—but you never would've recognized 'em unless you knew they were in there . . .

DAVE BARRY, the Desert Inn's "Hello America" comedy star, looked around the room at the above-mentioned Halloween party which was populated by the craziest costumes he'd ever seen, and said: "Instant LSD!" . . .

SAM SALERNO, KLAV, is in the army of believers that Rouvaun might be the world's greatest singer. He compares him with the greatest of the greats—Lanza, Caruso, etc.

★   ★   ★

JOE E. LEWIS, in his Aladdin show, says, "Arnold Palmer claims I'm the best alcoholic golfer because of my Canadian Club."

Billboard magazine, the Bible of broadcasters, came to Las Vegas in the fall of 1967 to do a story on show business, and to find out what the radio stations were programming for the local populace. We who were running radio stations were happy for their presence because it gave the nation an idea of what the tastes were of the locals; that Las Vegas was about more than gambling.

To the contrary, Las Vegas is any normal town away from the Strip. There were wonderful schools, many churches, areas, and parks where children could play, and golf courses to accommodate the golfer. In addition, there was Lake Mead for the fisherman and Mt. Charleston for the skier, just a few miles away. So as you can readily see, Las Vegas was about more than gambling. In addition, the Nevada Test Site was in full swing, testing the atomic bomb. Workers who made the trip had to travel at least sixty miles in each direction.

Another attraction to entice people to come to Las Vegas was Helldorado Days, which took place during the Sprin. It was a time when Vegas went Western, when employees in all endeavors wore Western clothes and looked and acted the part. After all, Las Vegas is kind of Western in its make up; a desert community with horses, downtown card rooms, a railroad station, and plenty of sand and dust throughout the year to give it the Western motif.

Billboard did well with its visit, because many of the hotels took out ads to promote their shows and venues. When it came to advertising, Vegas folks knew it had to be done, thus the great exposure worldwide.

Each station manager or program director was happy to receive the ink.

GOOD AND FAIR COMPETITION

It is unheard of in most competitive enterprises, but when a new hotel opened (during the 1953-65 era), it was not uncommon for Frank Sinatra to get together with Jackie Friedman, both representing the Sands Hotel, to venture over to that new hotel and give them a complimentary play at the gambling tables of over $100,000. Sounds illogical in this dog-eat-dog world of competition. For those who do not comprehend a complimentary play, it's where other hotels welcome the newcomer by stopping by and gambling to encourage others to do the same…this is what Sinatra and Friedman did.

You may wonder why a competitor would do this. In the early days, gaming operators knew there was enough to go around for all. The Sands Hotel wasn't going to hurt itself in this manner. Just the opposite. After Frank and Jackie did their thing, patrons at the new hotel would venture down the Strip or across the street, and head for the Sands to see Frank and perhaps the rest of the Rat Pack.

As I said earlier, Jack Entratter and Al Freeman were innovators in the world of publicity and promotions, and this was just another way of acclimating gamblers to a new hotel and at the same time promoting their own hotel.

Yes, there was enough money to go around to accommodate all the hotels at that particular time. Wouldn't that be great to see today? Stop dreaming, Sam!

When vacationers and gamblers came to Las Vegas in the '50's and '60's many patronized the Desert Inn because it was one of the first big hotels to appear on the Strip. The Strip, if you were not from Sin City, is Las Vegas Boulevard. The Strip portion, of course, is where all the hotels are located, and today it is still Las Vegas Boulevard.

The main man who everyone loved at the Desert Inn was Wilbur Clark. He received all the press and notoriety, but, in essence, he was just the so-called front for the boys from Cleveland - Moe Dalitz and company. Naturally, it wouldn't be known as Moe Dalitz' Desert Inn, or Allard Roen's Desert Inn, as the names wouldn't be appealing nor make sense at least to the general public.

Wilbur Clark was a perfect man who gave the impression he ran the show (hotel), but those in the know knew Moe and his Cleveland friends were the real decision-makers.

From a public relations standpoint, the ploy worked beautifully for years. Wilbur fit the part, received a great salary, and did nothing to harm the Desert Inn or its gamblers, preserving a good image for the hotel.

The Cleveland guys were good guys (at least in our town). They gave to charities and did all in their power to promote Las Vegas and tourism in general. At the time they employed Gene Murphy, one of the top public relations men in the country, respected and admired for his work in that field.

Having the Tournament of Champions on their golf course each year added to their popularity. Plus, Dalitz and Roen were avid golfers and drew the money players to the Desert Inn. The locals knew that Wilbur Clark was just the spokesman for the boys from Cleveland, and, stature or no, he was popular and well-liked.

It truly was Wilbur Clark's Desert Inn!

There was always a way to top a fellow broadcaster who had an ego problem, someone who was a little on the conceited side. This was the case with Jean Paul King, who at one time was the voice for Paul Whiteman's band, broadcasting from Chicago. He was big stuff in our business.

When he worked in Las Vegas he was at the end of his career and was living on his former exploits. Those of us who were in the profession tolerated him and his attitude, but we couldn't wait to get even with him.

One such fellow who was resentful of Jean was Robert Bock, my program director at KLAS (the CBS affiliate). He thought of a plan to upstage Jean. Bob had a great voice and could imitate many celebs and personalities. He called Jean Paul King imitating Edward R. Murrow. The conversation went like this; "Jean, this is Ed Murrow. I'm taking a sabbatical from CBS. I need someone to fill my spot while I'm away, and I could think of no one else to replace me than you. Do you think you can clear your calendar to take this position?"

Well, Jean went bananas and could not contain himself. He traveled all over town to boast about his new fill-in position on the major network . He called friends in the media to make sure they knew about the position he was given.

Meanwhile, Bob Bock was having second thoughts, thinking he was going to get into big trouble for the hoax he pulled, so he called to confess. But Jean didn't believe Bob. As far as Jean was concerned, he was going to fill in for the great Edward R. Murrow on CBS Radio. His ego wouldn't allow him to believe it was a hoax. Bock's comment: "Gotcha!"

Robert Bock married a Sahara Hotel showgirl and went on to work as a newsman at KRLA in Los Angeles and then on to Oklahoma City, where, before his audition for KOMA, he died of a brain aneurysm at an early age.

ROY COHN

One of the most controversial figures in American politics was Senator Joe McCarthy, who conducted witch hunts against politicians, citizens, and most particularly, the Hollywood crowd who didn't conform to his political party or beliefs.

McCarthy accused people of being Red Herrings or Communists and made false accusations about people's true loyalty. Liberals were his primary targets.

Many of those accused during this ugly era in American history lost their jobs and had their careers ruined. Some were even jailed. These verdicts were later overturned and declared unconstitutional. But some people committed suicide.

By McCarthy's side during these hearings was a young attorney who made a name for himself. It was Roy Cohn, and by virtue of these hearings, he became as well known as McCarthy himself. At a grand opening at one of the Las Vegas Hotels (Stardust), Roy Cohn made an appearance because of his friendship with the owners of the Desert Inn Hotel. He is seen here with Judge Zenoff.

Whether McCarthy was blinded by his own stupidity or ignorance just to promote his ideology, we will never know. But we do know that a new name emerged in the legal world. And that name was Roy Cohn.

LOWELL THOMAS

When I managed the CBS Radio affiliate KLAV, Lowell Thomas, the nightly newscaster for that network, came to town. He had inquired prior to his trip whether we could handle his broadcast from our end, whether our personnel at the station were up to the task. We had the right crew to fulfill his wishes.

His newscast wasn't 'rip and read,' as was customary in smaller radio markets. His newscast was written in New York and relayed via phone to my secretary.

Lowell rehearsed his copy prior to air time, and then he went on the air at 5:45 p.m. West Coast time. The newscast was set up in my office with Gordon Attebury, my chief engineer, supervising the broadcast.

Lowell and I became good friends, and after his newscast during his two- day stay, we made the usual tourist sights in Las Vegas.

In addition to his radio broadcast, Lowell Thomas was the voice of *Movietone News,* which was seen and heard at your local cinema before the cartoon and main feature. His voice was distinctive and very recognizable.

LOWELL THOMAS
HAMMERSLEY HILL
PAWLING, NEW YORK 12564

August 23, 1968

Dear Sam,

    You are indeed a wise man to move to Carmel. I hear you have sold KLAV to Howard Hughes.

    Sure, I'll be glad to do that tape for you.

             Cordially,

To show you what a great person he was, when I purchased KRML in Carmel in 1968, I sent Lowell some station breaks to record, and without hesitation, those promo spots were in the mail the following week. This would be unheard of today with agents, managers, and others who want to be paid for recordings of this nature. And perhaps too, some of the broadcast unions would put a damper on this kind of request.

When he returned to Pawling, New York, Lowell sent me some pictures taken during one his travels around the world. It was a picture with some natives, who were head hunters.

August 19, 1968

Mr. Lowell Thomas
Hammersley Hill
Pawling, New York

Dear Lowell:

A short note to inform you that I will be leaving KLAV at the end of this month and have purchased radio station KRML in Carmel, California. Naturally, the aforementioned is subject to FCC approval.

I hope to get a CBS affiliation and I trust you can put in a good word for me with Maulsby, Salline, and company. They appear reticent and won't commit nor can they until the sale becomes final. Their hesitancy is due to KCBS which puts in a signal there, although it is 120 miles away.

Years ago(50 & '51) I worked in Monterey when KMBY was the CBS affiliate and Bing Crosby and Kenyon Brown(the late) owned the station.

Want to thank you for your help and encouragement during my stay in Las Vegas.

Could you record a couple congratulatory station i.d.'s?

THIS IS LOWELL THOMAS AND I WANT TO WISH SAM SALERNO AND HIS STAFF

THE VERY BEST WITH K R M L, CARMEL, CALIFORNIA.

THIS IS LOWELL THOMAS, AND I KNOW MY FRIENDS ON THE MONTEREY PENINSULA

ENJOY LISTENING TO RADIO STATION K R M L, IN CARMEL, CALIFORNIA.

Best to you Lowell and drop a line.....

             Sam

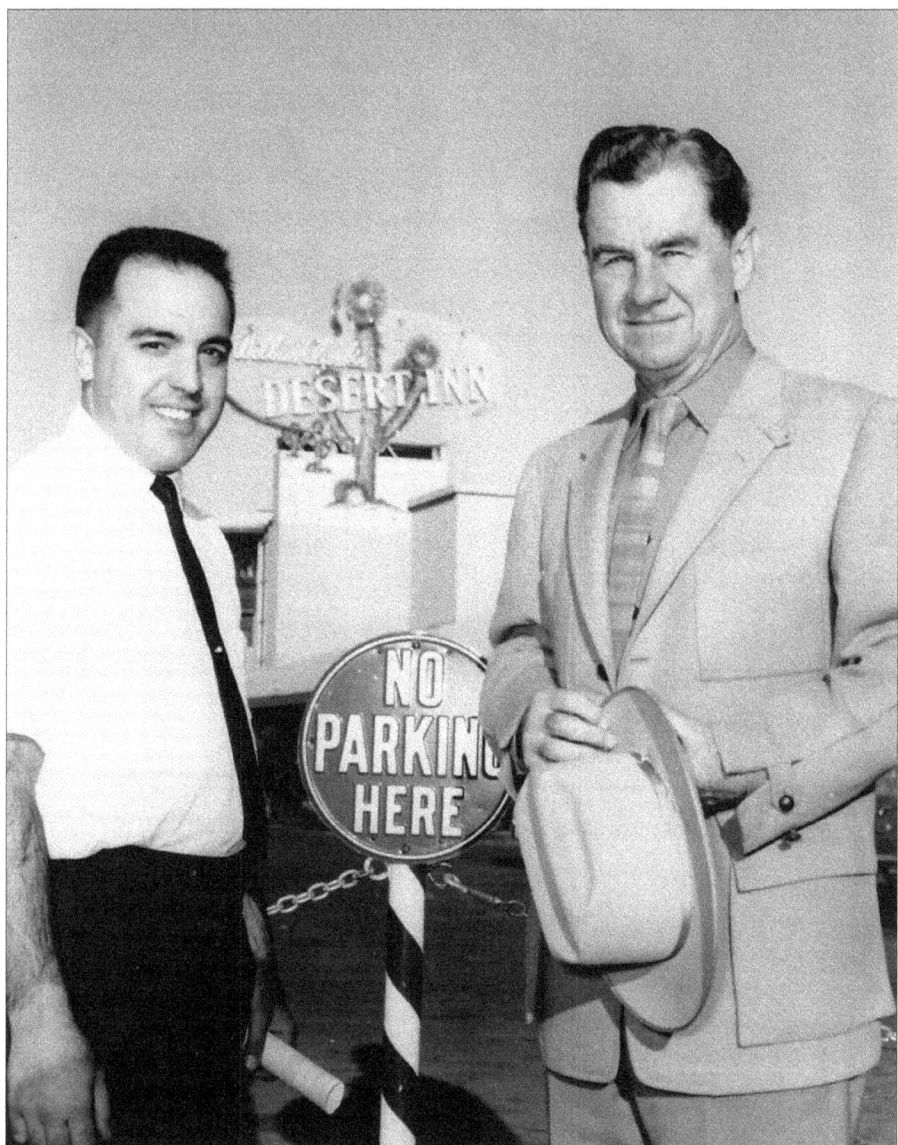

Lowell Thomas, famous CBS announcer and the voice of *Movietone News*, gets the royal Vegas treatment from me.

During my years in Las Vegas spinning records the money wasn't great, so one had to devise a plan to increase the revenue stream.

I had a good many friends in the business who were in fairly large markets also spinning records, but their audience was larger than ours in Las Vegas. The recording stars I interviewed on my morning show always wanted additional exposure to help sell their discs. So my plan was to get into the record promotion business.

My first client was Van Alexander, who had just released an album on Capitol Records. It depicted, in music, the Savoy Ballroom in New York. There were some great standard tunes on the LP, and I thought I could get Van some good exposure. Most of my friends were playing middle-of-the-road music and not rock or hard rock, so I had one foot in the door.

Van paid me one hundred dollars a week, and I began my new endeavor promoting records. Incidentally, if you didn't know, Van composed *A Tisket, A Tasket*, collaborating with Ella Fitzgerald.

My second client was Dorothy Donnegan, a jazz pianist who recorded on the Capitol label.

After Dorothy Donnegan, Lionel Hampton came aboard, promoting his new label, Glad Hamp, referring to his wife Gladys, and Hamp himself.

Art and Dotty Todd, whose hit, *Chanson d'Amour* was on the charts, also came aboard to get some national exposure for their records. When not recording, they appeared at the Top of The Strip at the Dunes Hotel, the same room that featured Russ Morgan and Freddy Martin.

All these promotions lasted from one to three months, but ultimately my new adventure didn't last too long, because I got into radio station management and that occupied most of my time. But it was a good way to make some extra cash.

During the early 50's and 60's there were many opportunities to meet recording stars, whether it was Jack Jones (a youngster at the time), Bill Haley and his Comets, the Lancers, the Four Lads, the Four Knights, Ella Fitzgerald, and many others. Having access to them was very common; the hotels wanted to entice radio listeners to patronize their hotels, and the recording stars needed exposure to generate sales for their new discs.

By virtue of my association with these recording stars, it further helped me to get into the record promotion business. As mentioned previously, it was a way to bring in more income.

Ray Conniff, a Columbia recording star, was quite popular at the time with his vocal singing group and had a number of hits, but there was always room for more promotions. Ray personally made the rounds to the various radio stations in Las Vegas whose format fit the bill. As you know, there were many formats in Vegas radio: Western, Rock & Roll, Classical, and Middle-of-the Road (MOR), which was our format at KLAS and later, KLAV.

Ray was also good about supplying the radio stations with product, particularly his long playing records. It also helped to fill the radio station bins with Columbia Records. One of his big hits which received a good deal of play on our station was *Lara's Theme* from the movie *Dr. Zhivago*. It went gold for this vocal group.

Today in radio, there is very little personal touch. You can download music from your computer, which has clobbered sales of long playing records and CDs. The more I think of what we have today, the more I remember what a treat it was to have the artist appear in person at the radio station.

When I was spinning records at KLUC (KAY-LUCK) in Las Vegas after my stint with Louis Prima, a gentleman came into the studios, which were situated behind the Frontier Hotel. He was wearing Western garb and looked like a real cowboy. He introduced himself to me and told me he was promoting a new singer named Vicki Sallee. The gentleman's name was Ben Kraft. He was part owner of the Thunderbird Hotel on the Strip.

Ben had one of Vicki's records and wanted me to hear it and determine whether it was air worthy for the station and whether it could be included in the format.

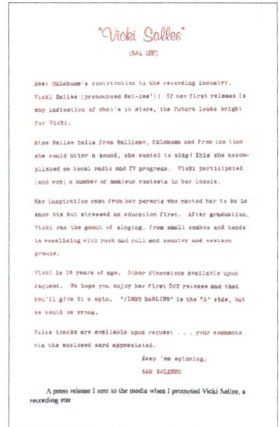

I auditioned the disc and informed Ben that we couldn't play her record on the station. It was a little rock-ish and not conducive to our sound. Radio Station KENO in the city was more of that flavor, I thought, for his client.

In our conversation I mentioned to Ben that in between my jockey shift, I handled record promotions for a few recording stars: These stars included Van Alexander, Milt Herth, the organist, Dorothy Donegan, jazz pianist, Louis

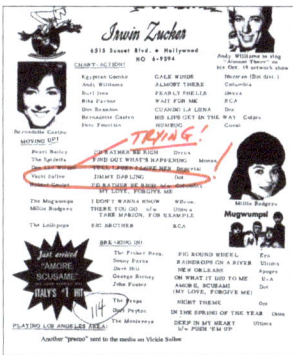

Prima, and Lionel Hampton. Ben asked how many records I needed (45 rpms), and I told him at least a hundred to send around the country to my deejay friends.

Ben Kraft went to his car, brought in the discs, handed me some cash (which I didn't count), and told me I could handle Vicki's record promotions. From that moment on I took charge of all publicity for her, which included sending press releases, and purchasing space in *Billboard* and other broadcast periodicals.

When Ben Kraft departed, I looked at the money he handed me and was startled at the amount…a cool $1,500. I nearly became hysterical, because I hadn't experienced this kind of compensation before, ever.

Ben Kraft was a good person, and if he believed in you, then the world was yours. This is how people operated in Las Vegas in the early days…everything in business was done with a good handshake. Money was never an object.

Revered as one of the greatest golfers ever to set foot on a golf course, that best describes Byron Nelson, the Texan who won consecutive tournaments during the War years of the '40's. Byron played many rounds as a youngster competing with Ben Hogan, who also hailed from Texas and caddied the same time Hogan did. Both respected each other's game.

Nelson was also a tutor for many golfers. One in particular was Ken Venturi. Hogan was also in Kenny's corner, and the three of them played many competitive rounds together.

I had the opportunity to meet Byron during the Sahara Invitational Tournament held in Las Vegas at the Stardust Golf Tournament. At that time, Nelson was helping Dave Ragan with his game and made a special trip to Las Vegas to check on his pupil. Ragan, a Florida resident, was one of top touring pros on the PGA tour.

The round ended as I was chatting with Mr. Nelson, and Ragan didn't appear too happy with his round; he made it known to Byron. Ragan said, "I only hit six shots today that I feel were hit right!" Byron wasn't buying it and retorted, "If you hit six shots that you feel were properly hit, don't feel badly. Now, you have to increase the number each time you play!"

What Byron Nelson was trying to express to Dave Ragan is to hit as many quality shots as you can. Some shots will be the result of the swing you put on the ball and will feel right, and others will not have the same effect. Try to have more of the good than the bad. Sounds logical to me, but then again, I don't make my living playing golf as Ragan did.

I thanked him for the interview and went on my way, but I'll never forget the words of wisdom from Byron Nelson, a great ambassador for the game of golf.

While I worked in Las Vegas, I had an occasional game of golf (if you can call it that) at the Las Vegas Municipal Course, where most of the locals played. I became acquainted with one of the top amateurs, not only in Las Vegas, but the entire state. His name was Jerry Hanweck and he loved hanging out at the radio station I managed, even though he had little interest in pursuing the profession.

Another one of Jerry's buddies was Martin Bohen, who was almost as good as Jerry on the links. They played at the Muni Course and others in the area, particularly when they were in a competitive tournament. I played with them at times, but I was no match for them. They were schooled in all the rudiments of golf, and I wasn't. I was busy raising a family, and when I played on weekends, it was for exercise and not to be a low handicap player.

I must confess that when Jerry and Martin wanted beer to drink, I got them beer (they were under age). They never abused their intake, lest I would never be their sponsor.

To add to their prowess, Jerry received a golf scholarship to Stanford University, and Martin got a scholarship to University of Southern California. While on the golf team he was known as The Jolly Green Giant because he was about six feet, five inches tall.

I don't believe either pursued golf after their education. I lost track of them after I departed Las Vegas to run KRML in Carmel.

A bit of advice for anyone thinking of becoming a professional golfer: If you are not shooting in the 60's regardless of where you played as a teenager, forget the idea. I've heard stories of players who think they can make it on tour and only shoot even par on their course. Forget it. Jerry and Martin were in the 60's every time out as teenagers!

Wed., Sept. 5, 1962   5C   ☉. ℋ. Examiner—Page 53

Hanweck Tops Golf Qualifiers

By PHIL NORMAN

Jerry Hanweck, an interloper from Las Vegas, stole medalist honors in the sectional qualifying round of the United States Amateur golf championships at Orinda Country Club yesterday.

Hanweck, a medium sized 19 year old swinger, who enrolled at Stanford University this week, fired a 74-73—147 to eclipse the San Francisco merchant prince, Bobby Roos, by a single stroke.

It means that Hanweck, Roos and the third qualifier, surprising Dick Keyser of the Claremont Country Club, will journey to Pinehurst, N. C. to play in America's premier amateur golfing classic Sept. 17-22.

TIMELY EAGLE

Keyser slid under the wire by making an eagle on the fourth hole of Orinda's hilly acres, giving him a 77-73 and 150 total. It allowed him to edge out William Farish Jr. of Pebble Beach, who needed 78-73—151 for the 36 holes of action in the wind of Contra Costa County.

Young Farish, also a Stanford student, will be first alternate and big Bill Higgins, San Francisco ink company executive, the second alternate with 77-76—153.

Ken Thomsson came along next with 76-78—154.

Main casualty of the pencil test was 17 year old Roger Maxwell, northern California junior champion who took a ruinous eight on the easy par four 17th in the afternoon round and fired himself out of the running with a 78—155.

FIVE SKIPPED

Another name player to miss was Dave Bohannon of San Mateo, who soared to 80 in the breeze of the afternoon and finished far back at 158.

It should be pointed out that five of northern California's finest amateurs, John and Dick Lotz, George Archer and junior 'stars Jim Welchers and Ron Cerrudo did not participate.

E. Harvie Ward, twice winner of the blue ribbon, will join Hanweck, Roos and Keyser as the Bay area's delegation to the National.

Ward has already departed for North Carolina, his former home, and is practicing for the gruelling event.

LIBERACE

As mentioned in a previous story, the marquee at the Riviera Hotel in the 50's showed Liberace the #1 star at that hotel and Barbra Striesand the #2 billed star. Well, as you know, that changed later with Barbra becoming a huge star and Liberace retaining his position in show business.

Because I was good with voices, the station asked if I would be interested in doing a radio show imitating Liberace and playing his records. I liked the idea and made it known that it was a go on my part. One didn't have to worry about lawsuits and the like, as one would worry about in today's society. The show came from our studios at the Flamingo Hotel, the first hotel on the Strip at that time.

I can't recall how long the show lasted on the station, but while it aired, it was the talk of Las Vegas. The listeners really thought that Liberace was doing the deejay show and introducing his own records.

Well, it was kick for me to do the show because I loved doing voices. In fact, during one of the shows, George Liberace, a good musician in his own right, sat in the studio while I imitated his brother. George was laughing throughout the entire show and it please me to see him going along with the gag.

George became a friend and sent me all his recordings. At the time, I took my first born, Michael, to one of Liberace's shows at the Riviera, and he was nice enough to sign a picture for Michael. In those days, it wasn't hard to get signatures from recording and motion pictures stars. Today, most are reticent because many turn around and sell the signature on eBay or the like. Can't blame them.

Liberace lived in Palm Springs and traveled to his gigs from that location. It was quite a mansion situated in an area off Palm Canyon Drive.

One of the perks of being a top disc jockey in Las Vegas during the '50's and '60's was to be invited to show openings at various Las Vegas hotels. In some cases, there could be two invites, or even three. In the early days there were three shows a night. Later the hotels cut back to two shows. It wasn't about altruism or taking better care of the stars. Instead, the bigwigs woke up realizing that you don't want to keep the patrons in show rooms when they could be in the casinos losing their money.

Those who were privileged had to choose some nights whether it was going to be a French show, a comedic show, or a top recording star. Those of us who attended were always given the best seats, usually ringside or close to the stage.

The publicity directors knew we disc jockeys didn't make a lot of money, and the waiters (whom we all knew) realized that fact. We still tipped from 10% to 15%, and everyone was happy. Those folks who were standing in line to see the shows were not happy with us, because we didn't have to wait in line. There was a line reserved for special folks, and we were part of that. There were times when the maitre d', to avoid upsetting the folks in line, snuck us through the kitchen and then into the main showroom.

Those were the perks of being a top deejay. Whether this prevails today, I don't know. Perhaps for the top TV personalities and top writers or bloggers, the comps still continue at most Las Vegas Hotels.

Following are some of the shows and invitations I received during my stint in Las Vegas, and I've never stopped thanking the hotels and public relations people for their kindness. It was a special time and remains in my memory bank.

A great
show!
Tony & Louis
at the
Riviera!

STARTING MARCH 7
DEBBIE REYNOLDS
STARRING IN THE
VERSAILLES ROOM

NOW APPEARING
in the

Fiesta Room

FRANKIE
LAINE
MAL
LAWRENCE

Hotel
Fremont

AL JAHNS & His Orchestra/2 Shows Nightly at 8:15 &
Midnight/Show Reservations: 384-3851/FULL COURSE
DINNERS $4.25/ MIDNIGHT SHOW MINIMUM $2.75

OPENING DECEMBER 21
in the

Fiesta Room

RED
BUTTONS

Hotel
Fremont

AL JAHNS & His Orchestra/2 Shows Nightly at 8:15 &
Midnight/Show Reservations: 384-3851/FULL COURSE
DINNERS $4.25/ MIDNIGHT SHOW MINIMUM $2.75

America's newest spectacular

PZazz! 68

A Hollywood Happening

DESERT INN HOTEL

STAN IRWIN PROUDLY PRESENTS

AN EVENING WITH

ROBERT GOULET

A NEW HIGH IN RESORT LIVING!

HOTEL SAHARA
LAS VEGAS, NEVADA

FEATURING . . .

THE MOST AMERICAN GIRLS IN THE WORLD!

JULIET PROWSE

as

Sweet Charity

RIVIERA HOTEL / LAS VEGAS

Eddie Fisher

mitzi is on the go

THE Riviera HOTEL
LAS VEGAS · NEVADA
Showcase of the World's Greatest Stars

FLAMINGO

THE SUPREMES

STILLER & MEARA

in the DRIFTWOOD Lounge
CLEBANOFF STRINGS

CAESAR BRINGS BROADWAY TO HIS PALACE

JULIET PROWSE
Sweet Charity
ELAINE DUNN

CAESARS PALACE
LAS VEGAS

NERO'S NOOK
RITZ BROTHERS
ROSARIO GALAN
BALLET
BILLY FELLOWS
MARION COLBY

extra added attraction
5th DIMENSION
continuous entertainment from 8pm

Theodore Bikel
Fiddler on the Roof

DOLORES   PAUL
WILSON   LIPSON

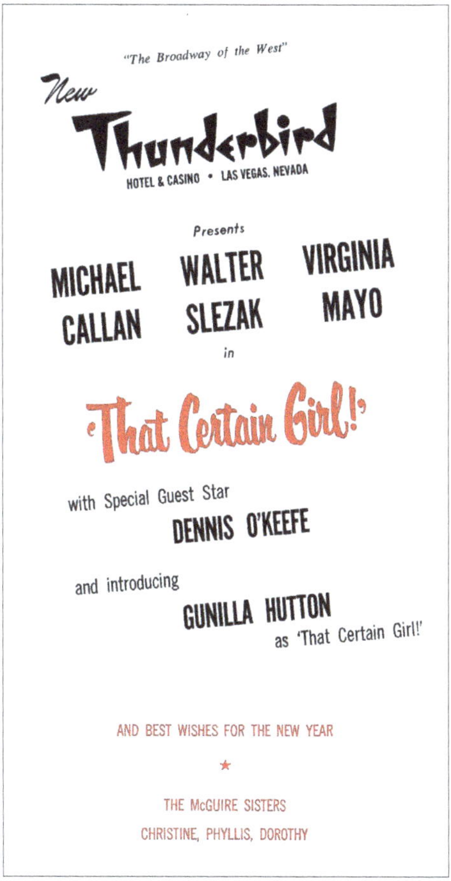

"The Broadway of the West"

New
Thunderbird
HOTEL & CASINO • LAS VEGAS, NEVADA

Presents

MICHAEL   WALTER   VIRGINIA
CALLAN   SLEZAK   MAYO

in

'That Certain Girl!'

with Special Guest Star
DENNIS O'KEEFE

and introducing
GUNILLA HUTTON
as 'That Certain Girl!'

AND BEST WISHES FOR THE NEW YEAR

★

THE McGUIRE SISTERS
CHRISTINE, PHYLLIS, DOROTHY

HOTEL SAHARA PROUDLY PRESENTS
IN THE CONGO ROOM
BUDDY HACKETT
and a PAUL STEFFEN Dance Production

HOTEL
SAHARA
LAS VEGAS, NEVADA

Jack Entratter
presents
in the
Copa
Room

Paul Anka

Marty Allen & Steve Rossi

ANTONIO MORELLI AND HIS MUSIC
· The most beautiful girls in the west · Costumes: Mme. Berthe
· Choreography: Renne Stuart · Lyrics: Sammy Cahn
· Music: Jimmy Van Heusen · Production Singer: Harry Nofal
· Orchestrations by: Albert Sendry · Set Design: Eddie Gordon
· Created and staged by JACK ENTRATTER · Two shows nightly—8:15 & midnight

"The Broadway of the West"

Thunderbird
HOTEL and CASINO
LAS VEGAS, NEVADA

PRESENTS
MONTE PROSER'S ALL NEW

Ziegfeld Follies

Showtimes 8 p.m. and Midnight
Third Show Saturdays 2:30 a.m.
(Adults Only)

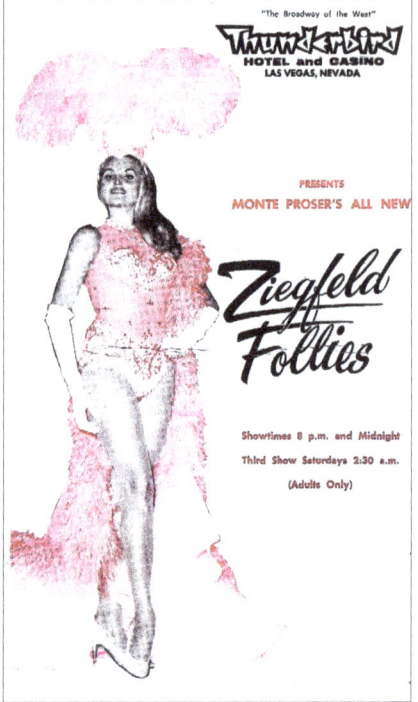

summertime is skeltontime!
Jack Entratter
presents in the
Copa Room
RED
SKELTON
DON FERRIS Conducting for Mr. Skelton

plus **LINDA BENNETT**

ANTONIO MORELLI & HIS MUSIC / The Exciting Copa Girls
Costumes: Mme. Berthe / Choreography: Renne Stuart / Sets by: Eddy Gordon
Production Singer: Harry Nofal / Production Orchestration By: Rob Turk
Created & Staged By: JACK ENTRATTER / Two Shows Nightly: 8:15 & Midnight

Opening July 27th:
STEVE LAWRENCE &
EYDIE GORME

The Crystal Room, America's Smartest Supper Club

Wilbur Clark's Desert Inn
Proudly Presents

SCENE 1

"Jubilee Americana" — The Yankee Doodle Gals: Carol Anderson, Rolande Beiber, Kathy Birmingham, Dion Bond-shu, Joan Boyd, Jean Carroll, Sharon Chayra, Dagny Duke, Lori Field, Carol Hanan, Shirl Hanley, Nancy O'Malley, Kay Martin, Mona Nair, Kathy Olsen, Beatrice Page, Valerie Perrine, Margaret Sbardella, Patricia Taylor, Denyse Turner.

SCENE 2

The Yankee Doodle Dads: Harvey Church, Ric Mitchell, Alan Riley, Ted Monson, Charles Fernald.
Miss U.S.A. — Folliott

SCENE 3

MAURICE
CHEVALIER

THE
KIM SISTERS

FRED STAMER, Pianist

Production number staged and directed by DONN ARDEN; Musical arrangements and Special Lyrics by Jim Harbert; Orchestrations by Jimmy Bryant; Costumes, Bill Campbell and Madame Berthe; Sets by Harvey Warren; Assistants to Mr. Arden: Bonnie Hunt and Bob Turk; Company Captain, Folliott Chorlton; Jewelry by Coro; Stage Manager, Jim Hawthorne.

Music for Show
CARLTON HAYES
AND HIS ORCHESTRA

SHOW TIMES
8:15 P.M. and
12 Midnight

Jack Entratter presents in the Copa Room

The King and Her-

Alan King

Antonio Morelli and His Music / The exciting Copa Girls
Costumes: Mme. Berthe / Choreography: Renne Stuart / Sets By: Eddie Gordon
Production Singer: Harry Nojal / Production Orchestration By: Rob Turk
Created & Staged By: JACK ENTRATTER / Two Shows Nightly 8:15 & Midnight

florence henderson

Opening
May 10:
DANNY
THOMAS

THE *Riviera* HOTEL   LAS VEGAS, NEVADA

REGENT 5-9111

May 17 1965

    Shecky Greene, the Strip's greatest lounge star,
is back in town.

    Won't you join us in the Riviera Hotel's Starlight
Lounge on Wednesday evening, May 19, at 11:45 PM for his
opening show?   Shecky will appear nightly at 11:45 PM,
2 AM and 4 AM until June 15.

    Please let us know if you will be with us on opening
night or if you would like to take a raincheck.

        Sincerely,

        "TONY" ZOPPI
        PUBLICITY DIRECTOR

NEW YORK MIRROR
DAILY AND SUNDAY

235 EAST 45TH STREET
NEW YORK 17, N. Y.
MURRAY HILL 2-1000

June 9, 1958

Dear Sam Salerno:

    Larry showed me your note regarding my Tropicana Show.
I was glad to hear you enjoyed it.   I was in great pain.

        Good wishes,

        Walter Winchell

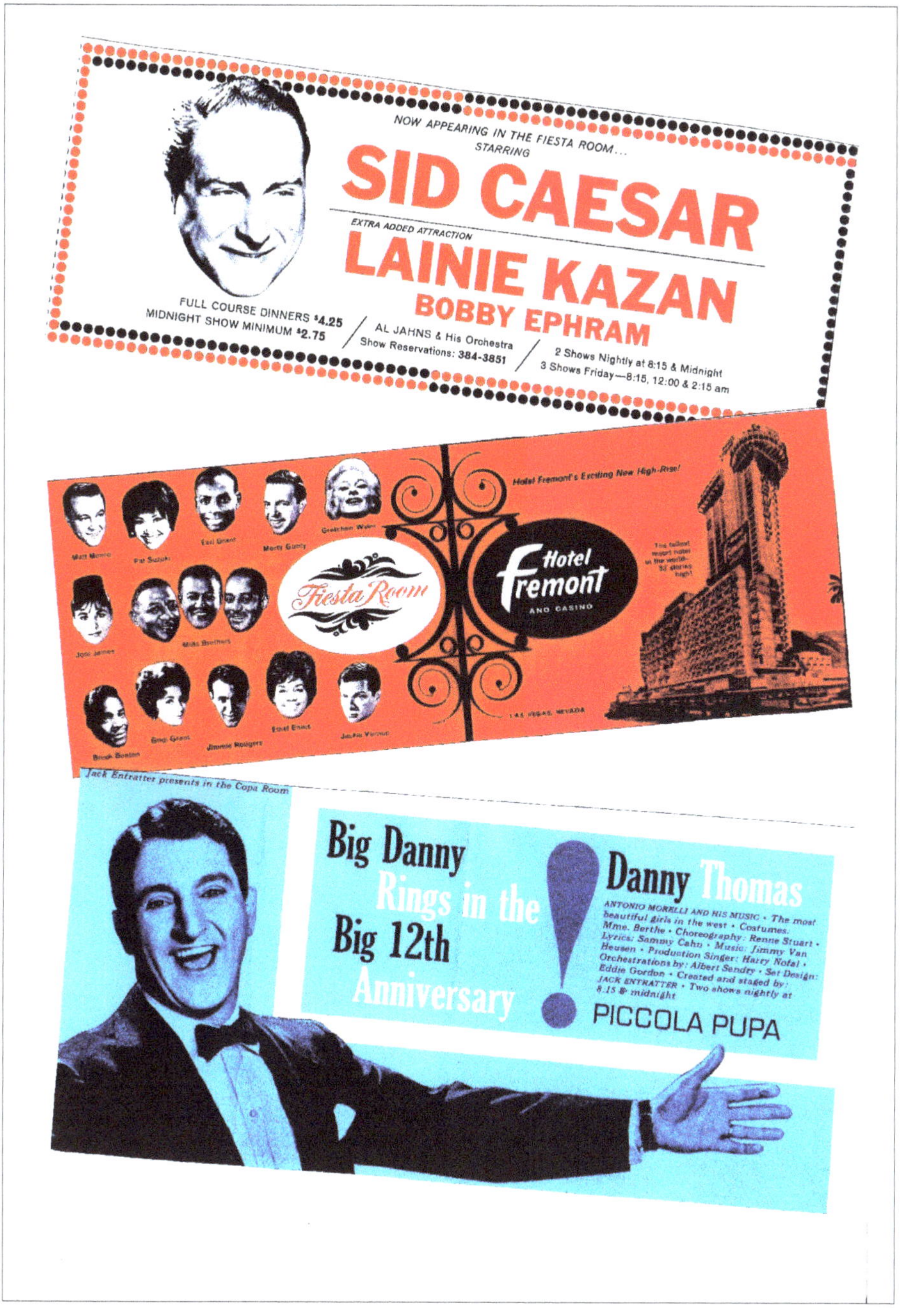

NOW APPEARING IN THE FIESTA ROOM...
STARRING
SID CAESAR
EXTRA ADDED ATTRACTION
LAINIE KAZAN
BOBBY EPHRAM
FULL COURSE DINNERS $4.25
MIDNIGHT SHOW MINIMUM $2.75
AL JAHNS & His Orchestra
Show Reservations: 384-3851
2 Shows Nightly at 8:15 & Midnight
3 Shows Friday—8:15, 12:00 & 2:15 am
Gretchen Wyler
Morty Gunty
Mills Brothers
Jimmie Rodgers
Fiesta Room
Hotel Fremont's Exciting New High-Rise!
Hotel Fremont
AND CASINO
LAS VEGAS, NEVADA
Jack Entratter presents in the Copa Room
Big Danny
Rings in the
Big 12th
Anniversary
!
Danny Thomas
ANTONIO MORELLI AND HIS MUSIC • The most beautiful girls in the west • Costumes: Mme. Berthe • Choreography: Renne Stuart • Lyrics: Sammy Cahn • Music: Jimmy Van Heusen • Production Singer: Harry Nofal • Orchestrations by: Albert Sendry • Set Design: Eddie Gordon • Created and staged by: JACK ENTRATTER • Two shows nightly at 8:15 & midnight
PICCOLA PUPA

More great stars appear on the Strip and downtown...Sid Caesar with Lainie Kazan...
Fremont Hotel stars...and Danny Thomas at the Sands

Andy Williams with the Omond Brothers headline at the Desert Inn.

WU015   O LGA484

NL PD WUX LAS VEGAS NEV

21

'—.

SAM SALERNO KRAM

RIVIERA HOTEL LAS VEGAS NEV

YOU ARE INVITED TO HELP ROSEMARY CLOONEY CELEBRATE

HER UMPTEENTH BIRTHDAY ON MONDAY MAY 23 AT 4PM OCLOCK IN

THE TERRACE ROOM AT THE SANDS HOTEL IT WILL BE NICE TO

SEE YOU THERE REGARDS

JACK ENTRATTER

WESTERN UNION

W. P. MARSHALL, President

LG188 DL PD LAS VEGAS NEV DEC 4 NFT =

SAM SALERNO =

KRAM LAS VEGAS NEV=

MISS THE VILLAIN CHEER THE HERO HAVE THE TIME OF YOUR

LEFE AS OUR GUEST AT THE SILVER SLIPPER CHRISTMAS PARTY

FOR SHOW FOLKS NEXT SUNDAY NIGHT DECEMBER 6 2:30 AM

SHOW ALL NEW REAL CRAZY MELLERDRAMMER FOR YOUR MERRY

HOLIDAY PLEASURE =

EDDIE FOX DIRECTOR OF ENTERTAINMENT

Tropicana Country Club

Mr. Ben Jaffe, President

cordially invites

Mr. & Mrs. Sam Salerno

to attend a

Club House Reception

Previewing the opening of

The Tropicana Country Club

Bond Road opposite Tropicana Hotel

Cocktails and Buffet

August 27, 1961   *Please present invitation*

4 p.m. to 8 p.m.   *Dress casual*

VU062(0LGA012) NL PD WUX LAS VEGAS NEV FEB 13 1956

SAM SALERNO

RADIO KRAM LAS VEGAS NEV

WOULD LIKE TO INVITE YOU TO ATTEND A SPECIAL INVITATIONAL

SHOWING OF MGM'S MUSICAL MEET ME IN LASVEGAS AT THE EL

PORTAL THEATRE 12 MIDNIGHT ON TUESDAY FEB 14. PLEASE

PRESENT THIS TELEGRAM FOR YOUR ADMISSION WITH A GUEST . THIS IS

AN ADVANCE SHOWING FOR LASVEGAS PRESS RADIO AND TV

PEOPLE AND CIVIC LEADERS. BELIEVE YOU WILL BE PLEASANTLY

SURPRISED. SINCEREY

AL FREEMAN

(745A)

WESTERN UNION
TELEGRAM
W. P. MARSHALL, PRESIDENT

0A517

O LGA706 LGZ2 NL PD=FAX LAS VEGAS NEV 15=

SAM SALARNO=   1959 JAN 15 PM 11 17

KLAS RADIO WILBUR CLARKS DESERT INN LAS VEGAS NEV=

PLEASED TO ADVISE THAT HOTEL SAHARA HAS INITIATED A "NO
MINIMUM" POLICY FOR SECOND AND THIRD SHOWS IN CONGO ROOM
EFFECTIVE WITH CURRENT APPEARANCE OF DONALD O'CONNOR, A
GUY YOU GOTTA CATCH. YOUR PRICE LESS THAN MINIMUM=
O'CONNOR ALSO WILL DO THIRD SHOW SATURDAY NIGHT. ALL
THE BEST=

HARVE=

WESTERN UNION
W. P. MARSHALL, President

0B377 SSR433

O LGA583 NL PD=WUX LAS VEGAS NEV 14=   1955 SEP 14 PM 7 46

SAM SALERNO=

RADIO STATION KRAM LAS VEGAS NEV=.

MILT HERTH AND HIS GREAT TRIO OPEN IN THE LADY LUCK
LOUNGE AT WILBUR CLARKS DESERT INN TONIGHT THURSDAY
SEPTEMBER 15 THIS IS A CORDIAL INVITATION FOR YOU TO
DROP IN AND HEAR HIM AND ALSO TO MEET HIM PLEASE LET
MARK SWAIN OF THIS OFFICE OR MYSELF KNOW WHEN YOU WOULD
LIKE TO COME IN=

EUGENE MURPHY WILBUR CLARKS DESERT INN..

VUO35

O LGY193 NL PD LAS VEGAS NEV 1-10-56

SAM SALERNO

K R A M RIVIERA HOTEL

HERE I COME INVITING YOU TO ANOTHER BIRTHDAY PARTY OF

MINE....THE 68TH....ON FRIDAY JAN 13TH IMMEDIATELY

AFTER THE SECOND SHOW IN THE OPERA HOUSE OF EL RANCHO

VEGAS

SOPHIE TUCKER

(325P)

WESTERN UNION
TELEGRAM

CLASS OF SERVICE
This is a fast message unless its deferred character is indicated by the proper symbol.

W. P. MARSHALL
CHAIRMAN OF THE BOARD

R. W. McFALL
PRESIDENT

SYMBOLS
DL=Day Letter
NL=Night Letter
LT=International Letter Telegram

The filing time shown in the date line on domestic telegrams is LOCAL TIME at point of origin. Time of receipt is LOCAL TIME at point of destination

1047P PDT JUN 27 67 PRB423
PR LGB173 LGZ1 LGZ1 DL PD LAS VEGAS NEV 27 NFT
SAM SALERNO KLAV
953 EAST SAHARA LAS VEGAS NEV
SOL W. GELTMAN VICE-PRESIDENT AND MANAGING DIRECTOR AND MIKE
RENIS-PRESIDENT AND CASINO MANAGER TAKE GREAT PLEASURE IN INVITING
YOU TO LARRY WOLF'S HOTEL BONANZA TO SPEND "AN EVENING WITH
LORNE GREENE" IN THE BONANZA OPERA HOUSE OUR SHOWPLACE OF THE
STARS ON JULY 1, 1967. COCKTAILS IN THE BONANZA CASINO BOOT
HILL BAR 7:00 P.M. DINNER 8:30 P.M. SHOWTIME 10:00 P.M. BLACK
TIE SUGGESTED. INVITATION FOR TWO. RSVP
    NO SIG.

WESTERN UNION
TELEGRAM

CLASS OF SERVICE
This is a fast message unless its deferred character is indicated by the proper symbol.

W. P. MARSHALL, PRESIDENT

SF-1201 (4-60)

SYMBOLS
DL=Day Letter
NL=Night Letter
LT=International Letter Telegram

The filing time shown in the date line on domestic telegrams is LOCAL TIME at point of origin. Time of receipt is LOCAL TIME at point of destination

236A PDT JUN 03 65 OB009
O LGA650 LGZ2 LGZ2 NL PD LAS VEGAS NEV 2
SAM SALERNO
KLUC RADIO NEW FRONTIER HOTEL LAS VEGAS NEV
PLEASE ACCEPT OUR INVITATION FOR TWO TO ATTEND THE FRIDAY,
JUNE 4 OPENING OF THE 'TOP O' THE STRIP' RESTAURANT AND COCKTAIL
LOUNGE ATOP THE 24-STORY 'DIAMOND OF THE DUNES.' DINNER SERVED
FROM 6:00 TO 8:00 PM WITH RUSS MORGAN'S ORCHESTRA AND ART AND
DOTTY TODD TO FOLLOW. PLEASE PHONE YOUR CONFIRMATION OR REGRET
TO THE DUNES PUBLICITY DEPARTMENT - 734-4617 - BEFORE 2:00
PM FRIDAY. REGARDS
    LEE FISHER.

4 0 24 6:00 8:00 PM 734-4617 2:00 PM.

WESTERN UNION
TELEGRAM

CLASS OF SERVICE
This is a fast message unless its deferred character is indicated by the proper symbol.

W. P. MARSHALL, PRESIDENT

SF-1201 (4-60)

SYMBOLS
DL=Day Letter
NL=Night Letter
LT=International Letter Telegram

The filing time shown in the date line on domestic telegrams is LOCAL TIME at point of origin. Time of receipt is LOCAL TIME at point of destination

808A PDT JUN 15 65 OB073
O LGA017 LGZ1 LGZ1 NL PD FAX LAS VEGAS NEV JUN 14
SAM SALERNO
KLUC RADIO NEW FRONTIER HOTEL LAS VEGAS NEV
PLEASE JOIN WITH PRODUCER JACK ENTRATTER IN HELPING SELECT
NEW COPA GIRLS FOR ENTRATTER'S SANDS SHOWS AT THE AUDITION
ON THURSDAY, JUNE 17 AT 3:00 PM IN THE COPA ROOM. KINDEST
REGARDS
    AL FREEMAN.

Rosemary Clooney

May 20, 1955

Mr. Sam Salerno
Station KRAM
Las Vegas, Nevada

Dear Sam:

Thanks so much for coming to the Sands
to be with me Wednesday night.

I appreciate everything you have
done in the past and will do in the
future.

      My very best,

      Rosemary

RC:BB

FREEMAN COMPANY

Advertising

Publicists

1/23/59

Dear Sam,

Thought you might like to have Frank's latest album
for your use and to play for your listeners.

Kindest regards,

Al freeman

THE SANDS HOTEL
LAS VEGAS, NEVADA
DUDLEY 2-7100

JIMMIE FIDLER

P. O. BOX 650

NORTH HOLLYWOOD, CALIFORNIA

August 16, 1961

Dear Sam:

Thanks for letting me know about Gene Murphy's surgery.

I have just air-mailed a note to him, and I am letting you know that I have done this.

Perhaps you have noticed that I use the names of his two resort spots in my programs quite often - but no other Las Vegas spots ever receive name credit. This is something that goes over my entire chain of more than 250 stations, and I do this for "love" of you and Gene.

Regards,

Jimmie

WESTERN
UNION

1 OB47B SSE5 20
1955 JUL 6 AM 8 20
O LGA666 NL PD=WUX LAS VEGAS NEV 6=.
SAM SALERNO=
    RADIO STATION KRAM LAS VEGAS NEV=.
YOU ARE CORDIALLY INVITED TO ATTEND DINNER SHOW
OPENING OF WALLY "WER PEEPERS" COX WEDNESDAY JULY
13TH ARABIAN ROOM 7:15 PM PLEASE CONFIRM WITH MAITRE D=
    AL GOTTESMAN DUNES HOTEL=.

WESTERN UNION
TELEGRAM

GA036 SSU115
O LGAOBO PD=WUX LAS VEGAS NEV 17 120AUP=.
SAU SALERNO=
    STATION KRAM LAS VEGAS NEV=
DEAR SAM THANKS A MILLION FOR THE SPINS YOUVE BEEN GIVING
FREDDIES AND HELENS RECORDS AND ALSO FOR THE WONDERFUL
REMARKS YOUVE MADE ON THE AIR ABOUT OUR WORLD PREMIERE OF
THE MUSICAL INSANITIES OF 1956 AT THE RIVIERA YOUR PLUGS
HAVE HELPED US BREAK ALL EXISTING RECORDS FOR THE RIVIERA
AND IM VERY GRATEFUL=
    SPIKE JONES=

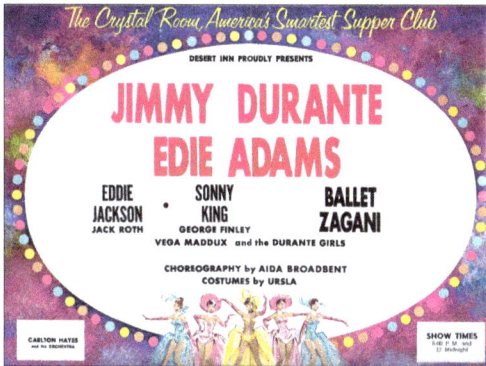

During the early Vegas days, dee jays were invited to show openings, regardless of who the stars were. As I've mentioned, the top record spinners and personalities were on the top list of invitees.

Gene Murphy, the Desert Inn publicity director, sent me a telegram (the custom then without emails and personal computers) to attend the Jimmy Durante Show opening. He was appearing with Edie Adams and Sonny King.

My children, Kim and Kathy, wanted to go that night, and I gave in. I couldn't understand why they wanted to see Jimmy Durante. It wasn't Fabian, Elvis, or Frankie Avalon. Perhaps it was to get away from home or to get some variety in their lives. Kim was a year older than Kathy; eight and seven respectively.

We went to the dinner show, which usually started at eight o'clock. Patrons arrived at seven, had dinner, and the curtain would rise at eight.

As with most Las Vegas shows, the entertainers put on a first class act, Durante strutted his stuff in dance and song, and Edie Adams ran the musical gamut.

There were never many complaints about food at the major hotels. It was always good. It had to be because these were the folks who kept the money flowing.

Prior to his single act Jimmy Durante appeared with the trio, Clayton, Jackson, and Durante.

I made arrangements with Gene Murphy to make an appearance backstage after Durante's show to have a chat with him and introduce him to my girls. We sauntered down the hall to Durante's dressing room, and Jimmy was there to greet us. Well, before any introductions took place, my daughter Kathy remarked, look Dad, he has a big nose! Jimmy Durante gave her a quizzical look and then chuckled. Guess he had heard those words before.

My face was as red as a beet, but I realized the comments came from a child. Again from the mouth of babes!

During my early disc jockey days in Las Vegas, that is, in the early '50's, I was approached by Bea Terry, editor-in-chief of *Deejay Magazine,* to write a column for the publication and tell all the things that were happening in swinging Las Vegas. Bea wanted to know what the radio personalities were doing, what music they were playing, and any news-worthy happenings that would interest their readers.

I was honored to represent Las Vegas and be their voice for this nationwide publication. Being on the VIP list with each hotel as a regular to be invited to most show openings, it wasn't too difficult to fill a column for each edition. This outlet also sharpened my writing skills, which needed honing in those days. Just like a good athlete, you can say that you can play a sport well, but there is something called performance and the same is true in writing. It was a great experience, and it put me closer with the public relations folks at each Las Vegas hotel.

There was also a close connection with the deejays in major markets, and this, too, helped me when I began promoting records for many performers who were featured at the hotels.

In the November 1957 edition of *Deejay Magazine*, there was a story about how Hugh O'Brian added to his acting repertoire by recording an album on the ABC Paramount label. In that edition, he asked the readers to give their opinion on which of the cuts on his "Hugh O'Brian's TV Album" they preferred. Ricky Nelson, Tommy Sands, Paul Anka, Richie Valens, Doye O'Dell, and Peggy Lee were just a few of the top recording artists to be featured in the publication.

Like most periodicals, *Deejay Magazine* didn't last too long; it went the way of many publications that didn't get enough national sponsors to keep it going.

It was another feather in my cap to be a part of *Deejay Magazine* while it lasted. The notoriety didn't hurt my career at all, and my relationship with each Strip hotel became better, thanks to the articles.

In his day, Frank Sinatra was considered one of the classiest men alive, and everything he became associated with shined with class. His attire, his regimen when it came to recordings (a perfectionist), and not your one-take, which was the word on Bing Crosby. He was in and out in a hurry, but the recordings were stellar. Sinatra would record until he felt the passion had been accomplished.

To go from one gig to another Sinatra flew in his *Cristina II,* a new jet with all the accoutrements of the latest in air travel. Remember, he went first cabin with anything he was associated with. *Cristina II* was used to fill engagements everywhere in the country, and it was used to pick up friends (Dean Martin), or family members when they requested it.

The reason I have some knowledge of *Cristina II* is the fact that Frank's pilot for this super jet was Don Leaetto, who befriended my brother Frank, a captain with United Airlines. As you know with major airlines, the pilots fly a few days and then take a respite, and days later, resume another flight. This gives the airline pilots time to do other things with family or indulge in a hobby.

Leaetto would give my brother a call and say, "We've got to go to Vegas and pick up Dean or Sammy," or any other Rat Pack members. So brother Frank was the co-pilot during these ventures and enjoyed the time with Don and with Sinatra. Naturally, he was paid for his time and talent, but it wasn't something that was compulsory. It was something done as a friendship gesture on his part.

I asked my brother Frank what he thought of the airplane, and it was a no-brainer: the plane was the top of the line, both interior and exterior, one that many CEO's and corporate heads used in their business.

Cristina II: another class act for Frank Sinatra!

As I've often said, doing radio gave me the opportunity to meet so many famous people. It was always a treat when a song writer came to town pushing his songs, which was no problem with me. Even though many of their tunes became standards, they still had to be promoted. At times, the music publishing firms and record companies were a little remiss in the promotion department. In all fairness to them, they had a host of recording stars to promote and not just one client. So we'll give them a pass on that.

Another song writer who I had the pleasure of meeting a number of times was Harry Tobias. He and his brother wrote many standards, and I admired their tenacity in promoting their tunes.

Harry's big hit was *Sail Along Silvery Moon*, and we spoke of this number when he appeared on my show. His brother Henry was promoting a couple of artists. Sinatra recorded their song *It's a Lonesome Old Town* on the album *Only The Lonely*. The Tobias' also wrote *The Bowling Song*.

In the late '50's, Keely Smith on her *Politely* album sang Tobias' hit *Sweet & Lovely*.

Many of the song writers were generous with gifts, particularly when I had my children. It was always a small check to buy the newborn something. Other times, we went to dinner or lunch. In my career, there was never anything like payola…that was reserved for the major market jockeys who could determine the fate of a new release.

It's nice to know that during my career I met some of the greatest song writers in the history of American music. Among those were Van Alexander, Herb Nacio Brown, Louis Prima, Ella Fitzgerald, Bill Snyder, Cliff Friend, and Harry Tobias.

It was a great time to be alive in Sin City!

I began handling Louis Prima's record promotions and publicity in 1963. It began first from Monterey, where I worked for awhile to forget an ugly divorce.

I handled his West Coast promotions and made the rounds to various top radio stations, those with the format that would conform to our kind of recorded music. I met with the top disc jockeys and hoped they would spin the Prima discs. At the time, Louis was well known and popular through his recordings for Capitol Records with his ex-wife Keely Smith. Sam Butera and the Witnesses were also known around the world through discs and short movie features.

I had entrée to the radio stations because I was a disc jockey before I became a radio executive.

From Monterey, Louis urged me to return to Las Vegas to work with his company, Prima Magnagroove Records, promoting singles and albums with his present wife, Gia Maione, Sam Butera and the Witnesses.

Louis was a good boss, but had little understanding of running a business, let alone a record company. There were many facets involved, and he was clueless because his whole life was spent entertaining and not running a business. He had poor advisors who really weren't in the mainstream of the music business. Previously, Louis recorded for Capitol and Dot Records, both of whom had fantastic distribution and a heap of money to exploit their artists and their work.

Well, to make a long story short, his company failed even though he had the best equipment and studio. His expertise was in entertaining and not in a recording studio trying to mix music, and to know what particular tunes to record that would appeal to the masses and create revenue.

I tried my best to promote releases through all the radio contacts I had, but his records couldn't compare to his Capitol releases. Plus, he didn't have Keely Smith on the label. Her voice and antics helped the group to become a hit. I resigned my position when I heard he was merging with a larger company.

prima POPOURRI

279 East Warm Springs Road

LAS VEGAS, NEVADA

It could only happen with Louis Prima, a show biz
giant whose name brings them flocking whether he
performs in a night club, theater, or on the screen.
Lee Burton, publicist for The Circle Arts Theater
in San Diego, where Louis and the group are booked
in February, called to inform us that the first night,
February 2, 1964, has already been sold out, and San
Diego is buzzin' anticipating the arrival of Louis,
Gia, Sam Butera, and The Witnesses.

In San Jose, the SAFARI ROOM is being renovated to
accommodate more patrons during Louis's engagement
there. If you think Chicago was a scene, "You ain't
seen nothing!!"

LOCAL JOCKS ARE TALKING ABOUT: "THE HOLLYWOOD HUR-
RICANES"! Their first Prima Magnagroove release is
out, and Coffee Jim Dandy, KENO's morning dandy, digs
both sides...that is, "HAVE LOVE, WILL TRAVEL" and
"BEAVERSHOT", but he prefers the latter.

Bob Joyce, Terry Randal, Tom Cross, and Don Adams
of KRAM also spinning the new HURRICANES release.
Joyce says, "They are refreshing," and has put them
on the KRAM play list.

PRIMA TIDBITS:
Bob Martin, KENO good guy, this city, leaves for
Honolulu to P.D. at KHAI. Sam Butera suggests that
Bob bring along his lawn mower! No word as yet on
condition of KFRC, San Francisco, music maker, Dave
Andrews, Dave underwent brain surgery.

ITEM FOR RIPLEY:
Our legman and runner, so to speak is Danny Secunda.
This name implies second! Well, we have "the first"
in our organization, and that is PRIMA. Now, we're
looking for a Tommy Terzzo. This would give us ONE-
TWO-THREE! Oi Vay!

The weekly "press" release we sent to publications, radio
stations, and all media outlets

Mr. Sam Salerno,
National Sales Promotor,
Prima Magnagroove Records,
212, Las Vegas Boulevard, So.,
Suite 12,
LAS VEGAS,
NEVADA,
UNITED STATES OF AMERICA.

BY AIR MAIL
PER LUGPOS
PAR AVION

Box 10872, Johannesburg

Louis Prima with Gia Maione
Sam Butera and the Witnesses

279 E. Warm Springs Rd.
Las Vegas
Nevada
89109

MAY 10, 1968

PRESS RELEASE

AFTER AN ABSENCE OF MANY YEARS, IN FACT SINCE THE "BIG BAND" DAYS, LOUIS PRIMA HAS RETURNED TO CLEVELAND AND IS APPEARING IN ONE OF THE MORE ELEGANT NIGHT SPOTS, THE VERSAILLES PENTHOUSE, HIGH ATOP THE VERSAILLES HOTEL.

THIS 9. DAY BOOKING FOLLOWS AN UNPRECEDENTED PERFORMANCE AT THE COPA IN NEW YORK CITY. THE PRIMA FANS WERE LINED UP FOR BLOCKS TRYING TO SEE THEIR "STAR" DURING THE CLOSING NIGHT. RINGSIDERS SAY THIS WAS A MOST MEMORABLE EVENING.

CLEVELAND PATRONS WILL SEE A "NEW" LOUIS PRIMA, INCOMPARABLE IN EVERY ASPECT OF SHOW BUSINESS. FROM THE TIME HE WALKS ON STAGE, THE AUDIENCE BECOMES "HIS". THE KNOWLEDGE ACHIEVED IN THE "BIG BAND" ERA PERMEATES IN ANY THEATER OR NIGHT CLUB APPEARANCE AND HE INTERSPERSES THIS WITH THE NEW SOUNDS OF TODAY...THE "IN" SOUND...."THE NEW SOUNDS OF THE LOUIS PRIMA SHOW".

MR. PRIMA GET HIS USUAL FINE ACCOMPANIMENT BY SAM BUTERA AND THE WITNESSES, FEATURING ORGANIST "LITTLE RICHIE" VAROLA.

MR. PRIMA AND COMPANY RETURN TO LAS VEGAS (THE SANDS HOTEL) ON JUNE 12th.

SAM SALERNO
PUBLICITY & PROMOTIONS

THINGS TO REMEMBER-
February 3rd--When coast-to coast TV audiences get
a glimpse of Louis Prima, Gia Maione, Sam Butera and
The Witnesses. Please don't attempt to adjust your
sets--the studio will be rompin' and stompin'!

IF YOU NEED PROMO copies of our records (LP or singles),
a note or a phone call will get the job done.

Later--

                    SAM SALERNO

METEOR records (pty) ltd.

AVON HOUSE, 127 PRESIDENT STREET, JOHANNESBURG
PHONES 22-6931, 22-5551 P.O. BOX 6049 GRAMS: "METEORDISC", JOHANNESBURG

13th February, 1964.

Mr. Sam Salerno,
National Sales Promoter,
Prima Magnagroove Records,
212, Las Vegas Blvd. So.,
Suite 12,
Las Vegas,
NEVADA.

Dear Mr. Salerno,

Thank you for your letter of February 7th. We are releasing the two LP's right away; "Prima at The Casbar" and "Thinking Man's Sax". When covers and discs are to hand, we'll send you samples immediately.

Can you let us have some biographical material on Gia Maione as well as some Photographic material of Louis Prima, Sam Butera and Gia Maione.

Please keep us informed as to your new releases and accept our assurance that we are very happy to be in the Prima Magnagroove "Family".

Kindest regards,

Yours faithfully,
METEOR RECORDS (PTY.) LTD.

R.R. MOSKOVITZ.
Sales-Director.

ED/...

DIRECTORS: A. MOSKOVITZ   M. MOSKOVITZ   R. R. MOSKOVITZ   F. J. LEWANDOS

February 21, 1964

Dear Louis:

It is with regret that I tender this letter of resignation. Last week some associates of mine from Hollywood informed me that you were planning a merger with another record company. I'm most happy that our efforts have payed off, and that the company has grown to a position of such stature. I'm only thankful that I was able to take time from my other activities, in order to get your record company operation on the road. I realise, Chief, that the remaining members of your staff are very limited, when it comes to experience in this field, so if you find yourself in a bind, let me know. I'll do what I can for you in an advisory capacity. Lots of luck. It's been nice working with you. Keep swinging!

Kindest regards,

SAM SALERNO
National Sales Promoter

A carbon copy of my letter of resignation with Louis Prima

LPE LOUIS PRIMA ENTERPRISES, INC.

270 East Warm Springs Road, Las Vegas, Nevada 89109/(702) 736-2046

Feb. 8, 1974

Mr. Sam Salerno
KBML-Radio
P.O. Drawer 5478
Carmel, Calif. 93921

Dear Sam:

We'd like to thank you for your many kindnesses and courtesies.

The opening at the Royal Sonesta Hotel was absolutely thrilling and really made me proud to be home again.

Kindest personal regards,

LOUIS PRIMA

LP/jh

Las Vegas REVIEW-JOURNAL

Tuesday, Feb. 25, 1964 LAS VEGAS, NEVADA Las Vegas Review-Journal 13

CAUSES FOR CONCERN

op LBJ Aides Frown er Threat of Inflation

Murray Hertz

Salerno And Louis Prima Part Company

PEEPING IN KEYHOLES: Long-time local Sam Salerno, seeking a possible merger with Louis Prima's record company and another recording firm (Dot, maybe?), decided to resign his position of National Sales Promoter for Prima. Sam, who was a popular local disc jock for many years in Las Vegas and knows nearly everyone in the business says he'll stay in town, possibly in radio and/or publicity and promotion. . . . Meanwhile, I understand that Fredrick Apcar has his own version of "Vive Les Girls" set for the Dunes Lounge in the middle of May—which scuttles the scuttlebutt of the Dunes' brass adopting a name policy in the lounge. With a successful French show in the main room and another French show in the lounge, it just goes to prove that these French gals have something that Americans dig. Must be the accent!

YOU'LL HATE ME FOR THIS, but it's a true story about schoolteachers drove in from San Bernardino for their first visit to Las Vegas. They became lost in one of the casinos and in their excitement they amassed a man's coats instead of a ladies lounge. There, adding to their consternation and to one of those fantastic coincidences, was a man one of the teachers knew.

Amid growing hysteria, she complained her friend to...

NEW SOUNDS OF THE WILDEST!
LOUIS PRIMA
WITH GIA MAIONE
SAM BUTERA AND THE WITNESSES
MARSH & ADAMS
THE SANDS PLAYMATES REVUE
SHOWS AT: 10:15 PM—1:30 AM—3:15 AM
in the Sands Celebrity Theatre

AGENCY PROMOTIONS (PTY) LTD
204 Pritchard House, Pritchard Street
Johannesburg Box 10872 Phone 22-0987/8

5th February, 1964.

Mr. Sam Salerno,
National Sales Promoter,
Prima Magnagroove Records,
212, Las Vegas Boulevard, 50,
Suite 12,
LAS VEGAS,
NAVADA,
UNITED STATES OF AMERICA.

Dear Mr. Salerno,

Ruby Moskowitz of Meteor Records tells me that he is busy signing a contract for the sole distribution of Prima Records in South Africa.

We handle promotions and public relations for Meteor and I would appreciate receiving "dope sheets" on all your artists and also photographs and sample records. Copies of your display material would also be appreciated.

What is the possibility of bringing, say, Louis Prima for a concert tour at a later stage?

Yours sincerely,

MANNIE HIRSH
DIRECTOR.

MH/lmb
DIRECTORS: E. BERSON, M. HIRSCH.

PRIMA PO POURRI

I've just returned from a motor tour of California, visiting stations and record folk. Nice to see Al Collins, Jack Carney, and Alma Greer of KSFO, San Francisco.

Dave Andrews of KFRC, San Francisco, back on the job after a touch of pneumonia. Dave is the son of motion picture star, Dana Andrews. Knows his music and is quite glib on the air. Formerly worked with this writer in Monterey, California.

Reaction around the nation to Gia Maione's (My-own's) recording of "LITTLE SIR ECHO" is very good. Dave Page, PD at KREM Spokane, tells us it'll be the featured record on December 7th. KCKC San Bernadino, has it on their daily "play" list as do KLAS and KORK this city. Incidentally, Gia is back with the group after a month's respite from the chores of becoming a mother. Might add that little Lena Ann is fine.

The "Chief" (Louie) has been inspired to write of late and has penned some fine tunes which will be recorded shortly.

Sam Butera's new LP cover is a "gas". But it's what's inside that counts! This without a doubt is Sam's greatest musical contribution to date. It is sensational! You'll be receiving your copy shortly.

Louie, Gia, Sam, and The Witnesses opened last night at the Sahara Hotel in Vegas. They'll be here til after the holidays. The Sahara has quite a line up at present. Buddy Hackett, Buddy Greco, The Characters, George Rock and company.

With the success of The Singing Nun, Louie and I thought it only appropo to come out with an album called, The Singing Rabbi! Could be a hit! Thirty ....

Sam Salerno

Another "promo" page we created for Louis Prima and his group

PRIMA PO POURRI

Another week of hot tidbits which has no bearing on the local weather. It has been hectic with temperatures hovering around the 30 degree mark. And mind you, the heat in my apartment was out during two of the coldest days. Brrrrr....

Speaking of temperature, Louie and the gang are the "Hottest" act in town! While other hotels suffer during this lull before the holidays, the Sahara Hotel Lounge is jumping, most of which is due to the histrionics of Louie, Gia (who is singing better than ever), and Sam Butera and the Witnesses.

Louie and company scheduled for the Palmer House in Chicago from January 21st thru the 31st. Tentative plans from Chi include Puerto Rico but this could be changed to a California engagement...bistro to be named when and if the deal is culminated.

Little Lena Ann Prima is a full month old today. Last week she was christened by Monsignor Collins at the St. Joan of Arc Church. The ceremony was performed in English and was the first in Nevada since the Ecumenical Council of the Catholic Church changed its ruling and allowed the priests to expound in English (or their native tongue) rather than Latin.

Reaction is still coming in on Gia's recording of "LITTLE SIR ECHO". Bregman, Vocco, and Conn, publishers of this tune are getting set for a big push in the New York area and think it could be their biggest song of the year.

More text from Louis Prima's corner

Whether I was in Las Vegas or on the Monterey Peninsula handling interviews it was always a delight to converse with the celebs, those in showbiz, and the sports personalities.

In Las Vegas, it was easy to have access to those stars appearing on the Strip, and the publicity directors made sure that the top disc jockeys filled their programs with interesting stars who could talk about their current shows or any new recordings they had in the can, so to speak. At times, we had to select from the various inquiries we received by the hotels about having their marquee stars on our show.

Appearing in town was the singer Connie Boswell who not only was famous as a soloist, but as part of the group known as the Boswell Sisters. In this particular case, she was working solo. Talk about a personality, Connie was just that; she had that special charm so prevalent among folks from the American South. Along with her charm and personality, Connie was a top recording star at the time. The year was 1954.

When I purchased KRML in Carmel, recording star and motion picture star Gisele MacKenzie was in town on a promotional event at the Monterey Fairgrounds. I had an opportunity to share a microphone with her. At the time she had a couple of hit records and was also doing a bit of film work.

I consider myself a lucky person to have had so many interviews, both live and on tape, for later playback with some of the greatest names in the recording and motion picture business. I was in the right spot at the right time!

I've been asked many times by folks who have never been to Las Vegas how the weather was in this desert town. Well, it ran the usual gamut from extremely hot to a chilling cold in the winter. If you didn't know, the elevation is 2000 feet, so freezing could be the norm at times.

Sand storms were prevalent at least two or three times each year while I lived there. If you didn't have proper insulation for windows and doors, you paid the price. Doors had to be sealed properly or sand would become part of your home make up.

Flash floods were common yearly when the city would experience three or four inches of rain in less than a half hour causing havoc everywhere, particularly for drivers. Making matters worse, the drainage system was obsolete and couldn't begin to cope with the rainfall. With so much rain in a short period of time the streets and highways were totally inundated.

One hotel which suffered the most during that period was the Tropicana and its Country Club, located just across the street from the hotel proper. With the downpour and deluge, the golf course would lose fairways and greens with each flash flood. Ben Jaffe, the owner of the Trop was not too happy and was after the county bigwigs to fix the problem because it was hurting business.

I can recall one such storm which found 30 or more cars floating in the parking lot of Caesar's Palace.

After much damage and consternation on the part of the hotel owner, the county solved the problem with a state-of-the-art drainage system.

As I said previously, the hotel operators didn't tolerate anything that interfered with gambling. If they had to contribute financially to solve any problem in the city or the Strip, they did so.

When I was pounding the pavement selling radio time, the temperature at the height of summer hovered around 110 degrees. Is it any wonder why I now reside in Carmel, California?

The Dunes Hotel on the Las Vegas Strip was synonymous with French shows in the main room, really spectacular presentations with most of the productions written and first shown in Paris.

In addition to the main show room, the Dunes had great lounge entertainment with a revolving stage; one group finished their stint and then the stage rotated, presenting the next group usually playing the same tune that the last group was playing.

At the l4th floor (Top Of The Strip), two great orchestras entertained diners and dancers. Russ Morgan and his famous orchestra would come in for a six-week period, followed by Freddy Martin and the Martin Men for the next six weeks.

Every second Friday, the bands would record two shows for CBS Radio sponsored by the Treasury Department. I had the privilege to be the announcer for the coast-to-coast shows and was treated royally by Morgan and Martin. They respected my radio talents as I respected their musical talent. Radio Stations KLUC and KLAV were the local outlets that fed the network these shows.

After I departed Las Vegas, the Dunes Hotel was razed to make room for a newer hotel. This also meant that the Dunes Golf Course would no longer exist because it was part of the entire property. Perhaps the new owners felt that gambling was more important than golfing. Well, it was more lucrative per square foot, which was what they were mostly about.

So much for the term 'progress.'

CBS RADIO NETWORK

NEW YEAR'S EVE DANCING PARTY

RUSS MORGAN ORCH. (DUNES HOTEL, LAS VEGAS)

SUNDAY, DECEMBER 31, 1967

2:00-2:28:55 AM, CNYT

ANNCR: Happy New Year, Mountain Time!

MUSIC: THEME UP AND UNDER

ANNCR: We're high on a man-made mountain - the Top of the Strip
           at the Dunes Hotel, Las Vegas with Russ Morgan and his
           Orchestra. Yes, it's Happy New Year in the Mountain
           States, happy dance time in Las Vegas, as Russ plays
           up a storm for CBS Radio's 40th annual New Year's Eve
           Dancing Party.

MUSIC: THEME UP AND OUT

ANNCR: AD LIB INTROS

MID SPOT: (INSERT MID SHOW)

ANNCR: Just a few more hours 'til Cotton Bowl time in Dallas!
           You can bet there'll be plenty of excitement when the
           Aggies of Texas A & M, and the Crimson Tide of the
           University of Alabama take the field. Hear every action-
           packed minute on this CBS RADIO NETWORK STATION this
           afternoon. Rick Weaver will be calling the play-by-play,
           Wes Wise the color sidelights. Your 50-yard line seat
           for the Cotton Bowl game, Texas A & M versus the
           University of Alabama, is available later today on this
           station.

                        (More)

           The script we used for the New Year's Show on CBS with Russ
       Morgan and his orchestra, at the Dunes Hotel, Las Vegas.

MUSIC: THEME UP AND UNDER

ANNCR: From the Top of the Strip in the Dunes Hotel, Las
           Vegas, we've been celebrating the 40th annual
           CBS Radio New Year's Eve Dancing Party. Maestro
           for these moments musicale - Russ Morgan with his
           Orchestra! Got the itch to switch? Don't fight it.
           We move 'cross town in the town that never closes ...
           to the SANDS Hotel and Louis PRIMA's Orchestra.

           (PAUSE) (CRN ENDS AT 2:28:55 AM, CNYT)

CRN: Driving? Happy New Year tip...avoid that extra nip!
           This is the CBS RADIO NETWORK.

           (NOTE: CONTINUE MUSIC THROUGH CRN TO 2:29:45 AM, CNYT)

       Script continues from the New Year's Show (circa 1967

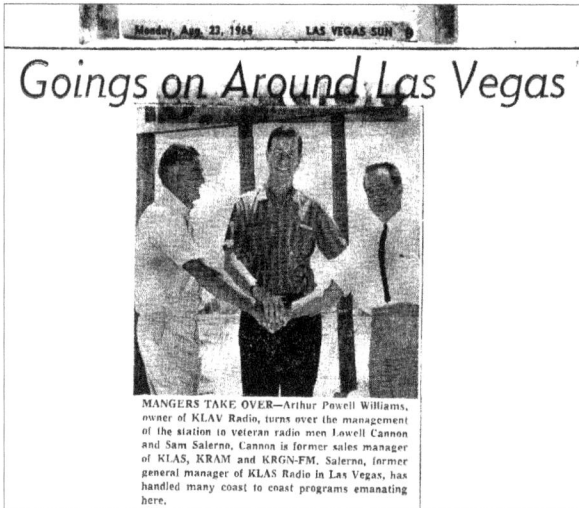

Monday, Aug. 23, 1965   LAS VEGAS SUN

Goings on Around Las Vegas

MANGERS TAKE OVER—Arthur Powell Williams, owner of KLAV Radio, turns over the management of the station to veteran radio men Lowell Cannon and Sam Salerno. Cannon is former sales manager of KLAS, KRAM and KRGN-FM. Salerno, former general manager of KLAS Radio in Las Vegas, has handled many coast to coast programs emanating here.

After a stint at KLUC, which was located behind the Frontier Hotel, and owned by the Gold Family, I was approached by Art Williams, the new owner of KLAV, to come on board as a sales manager.

I turned the offer down (this was in early '65), because for me to be successful at the helm of a station, I had to have full control. This was not an attitude of conceit, but my theory was that you could go all-out in the sales area, and then be stymied by some stupid decision from the station manager.

Lowell Cannon was with the station at the time, and we got our thinking caps on and decided to pitch the owner, Art Williams, on using us as co-managers. In August of 1965, Williams hired us as co-managers. At the time, it was a good idea for us, because we were both excellent salesmen and felt we could increase sales and improve the station's sound and image.

Cannon and I both handled radio shows, mine in the morning and his at night on the Cannonball Express.

There was no animosity between us, but the situation did not work out, and Williams decided that I was to run the station. At the time our sales were in the right position, and the station's sound was one of the best in town. Williams also promised me a share of the station, and I purchased 10% of KLAV. My wife at the time, Dee, was the accountant for KLAV.

I managed the station for three years, and then I had an opportunity to purchase KRML in Carmel. Mr. Williams bought back my 10% of KLAV. I departed for the beautiful Monterey Peninsula in October of 1968. Las Vegas was a great training area for my broadcast career. Having attended Monterey Peninsula College in the early, '50's, I wanted to come home.

KVIL Broadcasting, Inc.
2700 Republic National Bank Building
DALLAS, TEXAS 75201

August 27, 1968

Mr. Sam Salerno
P. O. Box 2963
Las Vegas, Nevada

Dear Sam:

I am delighted to inform you that the application for KRAM was
accepted for filing. I have only this morning been notified
and subsequently, pursuant to our agreement, please find enclosed our check in the amount of $2500.00 for the first half
of the Finder's Fee.

Mr. Oberfelder informs me that we should get quick action and
could conceivably receive approval some time around the 24th
of September. As soon as this approval is forthcoming, I shall
be delighted to forward you the additional $2500.00.

Jim and I would like to go on record as stating that we pay this
Finder's Fee to you with pleasure as we feel that you delivered
us a good property, with a good potential, and more importantly
were able to deliver us an extremely competent and capable
manager like Truman Hinkle.

I certainly hope we will have the opportunity to participate
in mutually profitable arrangements in the future.

Thank you.

Best regards,

Bob

Robert D. Hanna
Vice President

RDH:ds
Enclosure   No check enclosed.
            Called by tel.

When I received the finder's fee for helping sell KRAM Radio to the
owners of KVIL, Dallas, Texas

When I became co-manager of KLAV in Las Vegas in 1965, I made a deal with Dick Morrison of Spot Productions of Dallas to record station jingles. The jingles were part of our new station format and promos. The reaction to them by our listeners, who enjoyed the new sound, was quite good!

Before I resigned my position in 1968 to purchase KRML in Carmel, I received a call from Dick, who was speaking on behalf of Bob Hanna of KVIL of Dallas. Bob and his associates were interested in purchasing a radio station in Las Vegas, and they wanted to know if any were available. Who better to know that, they thought, than I.

Nice for them to have confidence in my knowledge of media in Glitter Gulch.

The deal was this: If I found them a radio property, I would receive a $5,000 finder's fee. Half would be paid when the sale was filed with the Federal Communications Commission in Washington, D.C. The other half would come if and when the FCC approved the sale.

I put my thinking cap on and deduced that there was only one station that was hurting and had an elderly owner who wanted to retire. That gentleman was former ABC executive, Ted Oberfelder, owner and manager of KRAM.

I went to see him and he certainly was interested in a sale; his price would be no lower than five hundred thousand dollars. Well, to make a long story short, the sale was consummated between KRAM and KVIL. When they took over KRAM, the new owners changed the format to country and western (C&W in more radio talk), and the station became KAY-RAM.

By this time, I was in Carmel at KRML when I received the second check of $2,500 for the finder's fee. Ironically, the new manager was Truman Hinkle, who was part owner of KRAM in 1953 with Ed Jansen. What a coincidence!

THE MONTEREY PENINSULA

MY CHILDREN

Like most parents, I'm proud of the children who carry my name, even though the name has been tossed around in divorce proceedings.

My first-born was Michael, who was born in 1956, raised a portion of his life in Las Vegas, and later on the Monterey Peninsula, along with sisters Kim and Kathy who are two and three years Mike's junior. They too spent years in Las Vegas, then in Carmel, and later with their mother in Livermore, California.

Sam Jr. was born in Las Vegas in 1965, lived only three years in Las Vegas and the rest of his life in Carmel. A fifth child, Sean, was born in 1971 and was raised in Lafayette, California.

Sam Jr. and Sean both have been educated, and each has a Master's degree. Sam has two Master's degrees, one from London University, and another from Weslyan University in Middletown, Connecticut. Sean's Master's degree is from the University of California at Berkeley. Michael attended Monterey Peninsula College, Chabot College, and UNLV in Las Vegas.

Kim and Kathy have worked at Intel and Lawrence Radiation Center, in Livermore.

Living in Carmel and doing a live radio show each Saturday for the past twelve years has prevented me from doing much traveling. So, in most cases, my children have to come visit their Dad.

It is my hope that they are successful in whatever endeavor they pursue, and when I can help, I do. Isn't that the job of a parent?

In the early '60's I spent a little time with KDON Radio with their main studios in Salinas, California. To generate more sales over and above those garnered in Salinas, I set up a sales office in the San Carlos Hotel in downtown Monterey, 25 miles west and on the coast.

In my travels around town, I met Elsie Walters, who wanted to write a short book giving energetic people (particularly women) a chance to repair an old hat and give it new life.

In her day Elsie was one of the most popular hat makers in the San Francisco Bay area. She was inspired as a child making dresses for her own dolls. She started at the Art Institute of Chicago, and atttended the Lucien Labaudt School in San Francisco. Her first millinery shop was in Oakland. Another shop was on Nob Hill in San Francisco.

She came to the Monterey Peninsula in 1952 and never left. Prior to that, she was lured to Hollywood, where she established a school of millinery.

We worked together on the book's publication, me doing most of the typing (no computers then). It wasn't easy. Elsie was a tough perfectionist. Luckily, it was only an instructional book and not a 300-page novel. I don't think I could have lasted with a larger project.

But to me, it was a start in putting words down to be published in book form. Its appeal was for those interested into turning old hats into new ones!

Hang on to Your Hat!

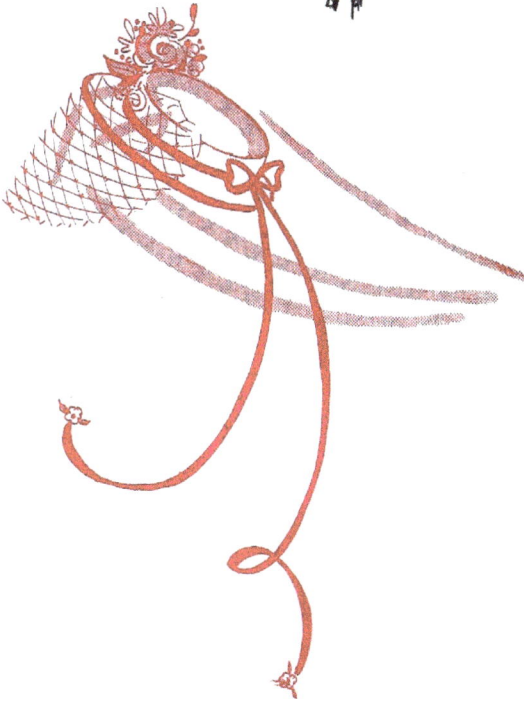

Elsie Walter

During the early '50's I worked at KMBY in Monterey as a disc jockey. Our main studios were located in the San Carlos Hotel in downtown Monterey. That hotel is now the Marriott.

KMBY'S transmitter site was on Wharf #2 but at this writing is no longer located there. It was pretty hard spinning records during storms because the waves would smash up against the pilings and cause the

needle to skip on long playing records or 78 rpms. Directly across from the old site is the popular eating establishment,The Sandbar and Grill, owned by Craig Ling.

Radio duties at that time were spinning records, doing a bit of news, and some remote broadcasts. On occasion, some sports reporting or news casting was thrown in at KMBY. The station was owned by John Miner, a Mormon from Utah. John was a good operator and a giving person.

One of the announcers on our staff was a tall red-headed Irishman whose name was Tom Sheehy. Tom was from the East Coast and a great, fun guy to be around. This market was too small for him, so he went to New York and got a job with CBS, not as announcer. But having a First Phone license, he handled engineering chores.

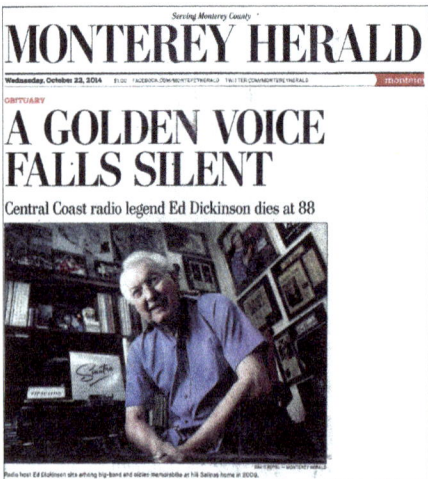

Tom and I kept in touch. Later in his CBS career, he was Arthur Godfrey's engineer.

When I was selected to announce *The Mitch Miller Show* on CBS from the Sands Hotel with the McGuire Sisters, Tom taped the show and sent me a copy. Nice to have friends in the right spots!

One of my co-workers at KMBY was Ed Dickinson, who later became a household name for his radio show called *Way Back Now.*

Long before Clint Eastwood purchased the Mission Ranch property in Carmel, The Barn was the place where big bands played and special events were held.

It was the early '50's, when I was a member of the KMBY radio staff, and I was called upon to handle a remote broadcast emanating from The Barn.

The music group was Jack Mathis and his band with southern singer, Dudley Nix, who could handle both the downhome tunes and Dixieland favorites. His style was that of song writer Johnny Mercer, the man who penned over a thousand songs, many of them American standards. When Dudley wasn't singing and entertaining, he was running a dance studio on Mission Street, two blocks from Ocean Avenue. The gig by Mathis and company was a one-shot deal and not a regular happening, as were most of the events at the Mission's Barn.

After this broadcast, KMBY began regular nightly shows from the Gold Room at the San Carlos Hotel in downtown Monterey. It was music for dancing and listening and popular in that era when dancing was the thing to do for entertainment. After all, TV was just beginning to make its mark on the nation.

The group was called Jose Flores and his Pan American Trio with Jose at the drums, Claire Norsen on the keyboard, and Johnny Catalano on sax, clarinet, and oboe. Catalano was recognized by musical experts and critics as one of best reed men in the country. Many big bands were after his services, but Catalano did not want to leave the beautiful Monterey Peninsula. This has also been the case with Peninsula athletes who have turned down professional jobs because of their love for this area.

Catalano is now playing those instruments in the big band in the sky. His wife, Rose, runs the restaurant they both started in Monterey called Cibo's, with the help of family members.

Clint Eastwood and his staff still accommodate private parties, weddings, class reunions, and other functions in The Barn. It's on everyone's visit list.

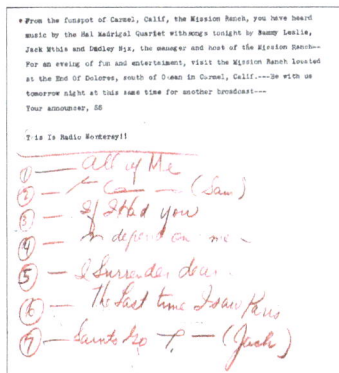

For an area that isn't too large in population, the Monterey Peninsula has produced some great athletes. One great known to sports aficionados was Ron Rivera, who went from being a top local athlete to achieve greatness in the NFL as a coach.

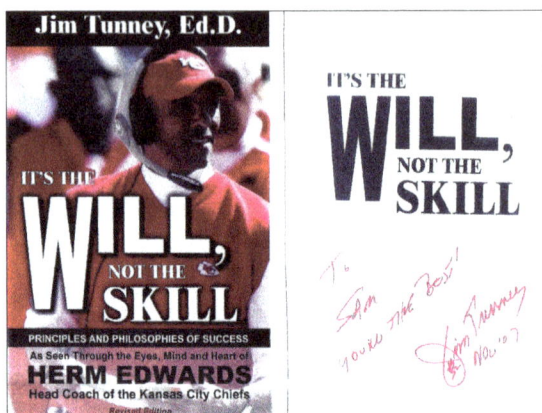

And then there is Herm Edwards. After a stint at the University of California at Berkeley, Herm came to Monterey Peninsula College, where he was a football star, among his many talents. He received the Most Valuable Player award in football, and was named the team's best defensive back. Later, Herm was also a standout as a professional football player and received many accolades for work ethics and raw ability and talent.

Golden Helmet Award

Monterey Peninsula College defensive back Herman Edwards (left) receives the Golden Helmet Award from Lobo Club vice president Eddie Esteban at the MPC fall sports banquet at Rancho Canada Golf Club last night. The award is given by Coca-Cola to the most valuable football player at each school.

Edwards, Pelton, Banker Named MVPs at MPC

Herman Edwards, Tom Pelton and Ken Banker received the Most Valuable Player Awards for their respective sports of football, cross country and water polo at the Monterey Peninsula College fall sports banquet last night at Rancho Canada Golf Club.

The Lobo Boosters Club sponsored the dinner, which was attended by 113 persons.

Edwards also was presented a trophy for his Golden Helmet Award given by Coca-Cola to the top football player at each school. This is the first time it has been awarded at MPC. Edwards also was named the team's best defensive back.

Those two awards were voted by his teammates as were the honors of top offensive back to quarterback Tom Craft, best defensive lineman to Steve Powers and best offensive lineman to Calvin Krebs.

Two special Coaches Awards, designated by head coach Luke Phillips and his staff, were presented for "personal achievement and development" to lineman John Careaga and running back Charles Smith.

Fullback Herb Lusk received the Boosters Club Award for being the Most Inspirational Player.

Besides being named the cross country Most Valuable Runner, Pelton also was chosen as captain by his teammates.

Other harrier awards presented by coach Dave Stern were to Andy Mozal as the Most Inspirational, Mark Jensen as the Most Improved and Emil Magallanes, the 100 per cent award.

Water polo coach Ted Trendt gave out the MVP trophy to Banker and one to Jim Leonard as the Outstanding Defensive Player.

The Circle K, a college level Kiwanis group, donated a perpetual trophy to the school on which the names of the MVPs of each sport will be inscribed each year.

Sam Salerno, owner of KRML radio and sportscaster on KMST-TV-46, was the master of ceremonies. President of the Boosters Club is Bob Massaro.

After playing, Herm was a coach for the New York Jets and the Kansas City Chiefs. Then he became one of the top sports analysts for ESPN, and at this writing he still retains that position. Herm is also called upon to give motivational speeches, and in those presentations, he relates his own experiences growing up on the Monterey Peninsula, and the tutelage he received from his military dad who was a great disciplinarian.

Although his position with ESPN requires a good deal of his attention, Herm still sets aside time to conduct his own golf tournament each year to raise money for local charities.

Herm Edwards is an inspiration to all young men, proving that with hard work and a great attitude, one can succeed as he has. The Monterey Peninsula is proud to have him as an ambassador for this great area.

In the early '50's while I was working at KMBY, I decided to continue my education by enrolling at Monterey Peninsula College (MPC). Naturally, I took a class in writing, which was a subject I enjoyed. I also took a music class and sang in the school choir.

El Yanqui — Vol. 5, No. 3 — Monterey Peninsula College, Monterey, California — Friday, Oct. 17, 1952

MPC Students Local Disc Jockeys

Salerno and Adams

Johnny Adams, who I trained to enter the broadcasting field after he matriculated at the Don Martin School of Radio Arts in Hollywood, also decided to take additional classes at MPC.

Johnny and I enjoyed our time at MPC, getting involved in the chorus, emceeing shows, and learning what the school was all about. A student, with whom I later became good friends was Larry Segovia, perhaps one of the best all-around athletes ever to come from the Monterey area. He was a great football player, fabulous baseball player, and held his own at basketball and golf. In the minor leagues, one of his teammates at Portland was Maury Wills, a name most baseball followers recognize.

After his sporting career, Larry opened up Segovia's Bar in New Monterey, California.

While Johnny and I were at MPC, we wrote a number of articles, one of which was our take on a proposed freeway which would run close to the school's location.

The time spent at MPC was great for one's ego. After all, we were radio stars (if you'll pardon the expression) going to college with the rest of the new high school grads.

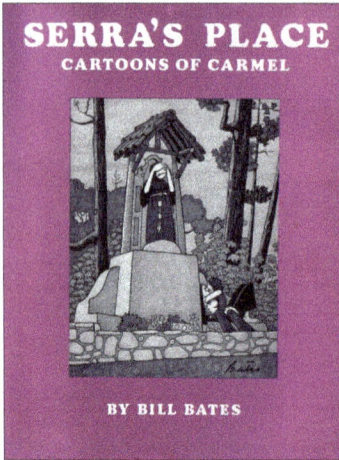

SERRA'S PLACE
CARTOONS OF CARMEL

BY BILL BATES

Carmel has been famous for a century as an artist colony, and the home of great writers, professors, actors, and every facet of academia. The trend still continues, though to a lesser degree because many of the greats have left us.

Among the cartoonists – yes, they are certainly artists – who have resided here are Hank Ketcham, Eldon Didini, Gus Ariola, and Bill Bates. I knew all of them except Ketcham. The closest friend among them was Bill Bates, whose cartoons are part and parcel of Carmel's fabric.

Bill was one of the most prolific cartoonists to grace the Carmel area. Everyone in Carmel knew Bill and his cartoons featured many of the townspeople, and, at times, the business community.

Like many artists, Bates was not a good business man, and many times he literally gave his art away. I maintained from the time I first met him in the early 70's, if he had hired a good business manager who could capitalize on him and his art, he would have been a millionaire. But, that was not the case.

KRML, Bill, and I, through a sales emissary, decided to publish a cartoon map of Carmel with Bill handling the art for the project, interspersing his art humor in this map. The year was 1975. Bates was paid for his art, we formed a corporation, which included his mother, and within six months he backed out of the arrangement. To this day, I don't know why, but we remained friends.

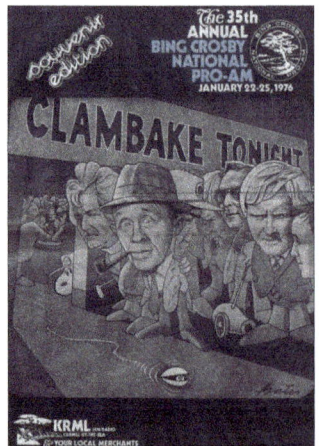

I tried to promote the map as best I could but it was never a big seller, even though I feel it was one of Bill's greatest works. Bill also produced some cartoon magazines, depicting many of the works featured in his weekly cartoon in the local newspaper. One of his cartoons (a cover production) was featured in a Bing Crosby Pro-Am tabloid which I produced.

Bates would take yearly cruises, and he would paint, cartoon style, some of the passengers. Later, he would convert these pictures into a book. He lived in Capetown

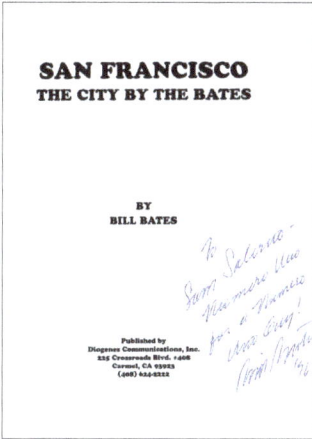

SAN FRANCISCO
THE CITY BY THE BATES

BY
BILL BATES

Published by
Diogenes Communications, Inc.
225 Crossroads Blvd. #408
Carmel, CA 93923
(408) 624-2222

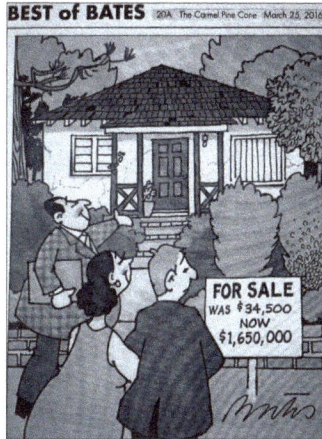

BEST of BATES   20A The Carmel Pine Cone March 25, 2016

FOR SALE
WAS $34,500
NOW
$1,650,000

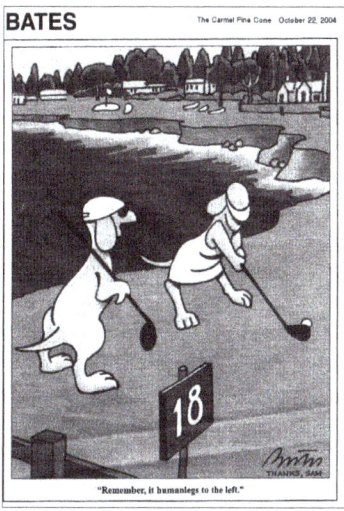

BATES   The Carmel Pine Cone October 22, 2004

18

"Remember, it humanlegs to the left."
THANKS, SAM

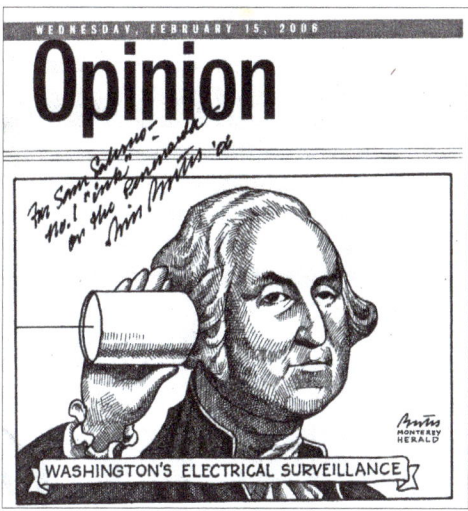

WEDNESDAY, FEBRUARY 15, 2006

Opinion

WASHINGTON'S ELECTRICAL SURVEILLANCE

MONTEREY
HERALD

for a while. To stay, the South African officials said he would have to employ six people. When he related this to me I asked, "What, to hold your easel?"

Yes, with a proper manager, Bill Bates would be wealthy and world renown.

Bates' cartoons (in book form) are still available at local book stores, and some of his classic cartoons are a visual feature at the Carmel Post Office.

Bill had a heart attack, went to the local hospital, got a staph infection, went into a coma, and never recovered.

Our cartoon map (circa 1975), his cartoon books, and all his creations, along with those of Dedini and Ariola, will live on. Perhaps soon, another crop of talented artist will make Carmel their home.

Little did one realize that Glenn Miller's brother, Herb, lived on the Monterey Peninsula near the Pacific Grove Golf Course and that he, too, was a great musician. Indeed, most of the members of his family were musical and played in his band. Their venues included the Mark Thomas Inn in Monterey, and the Madonna Inn in San Luis Obispo, to name just a couple of locations where their sounds were heard.

The types of music played by Herb's band were the same that made the Miller name popular in the late '30's and '40's, before Glenn donned a uniform for Uncle Sam.

I was approached by Herb to book his band if I could. I suggested that the ballroom at the San Carlos Hotel would be ideal, and we got the wheels in motion for the band to perform for the dancing crowd. The arrangements were made with Mr. Elves, owner and manager of the San Carlos Hotel.

The band played to a good crowd which could have been a lot larger, but if you haven't booked musical groups in this area, one doesn't know the problems. Some unknown groups packed them in, and others just don't make it. As an example, when I owned KRML we booked the Joy of Cooking at the Fairgrounds and made a goodly amount. The following week we featured the group Stoned Ground, which was popular at the time, and we lost money.

The Herb Miller booking was not a money maker, but it was great to hear the Miller sound and see folks dancing.

Herb Miller later moved from Pacific Grove to England, and we never heard another word from him. Quite a transition, I'd say, Monterey Peninsula to England.

It was just before the 1977 National PGA Golf Tournament, which was to be played at Pebble Beach, a great venue for one of the most prestigious tournaments on tour.

During this period, Olin Dutra, born and raised in Monterey, was teaching golf at Pajaro Golf Course in Watsonville, just a few miles from the Peninsula. I thought it apropos to take a trip to where he was teaching and extract some information from Olin, who was good with words and terrific with his golf clubs. After all, he would know about the PGA Tournament because he had captured the trophy 45 years earlier in 1932.

Olin was cordial, and we taped the interview to be used in a tabloid publication that I produced to coincide with the tournament itself. Olin said he got his start in golf as a caddie at Del Monte Golf Course, the oldest course West of the Mississippi. Olie told me, "We dug the game out of the ground, and we shagged balls and caddied for Mac Donald Smith, the pro at the Del Monte course, and we received 35 cents a day (this was in the '30's), and having been taught to be frugal by our dad, who was a laborer, we'd put ten cents away."

Dutra was just one of a long list of good golfers who received their starts in Monterey. There were the four Espinosa brothers: Abe, Al, Henry, and Romeo. Others included the Abregos, and Henry and Cam Puget. There are two streets named for these golfers - one for the Abregos and one for the Dutras in Monterey.

Olin finished sixth in the U.S. Open the same year he won the PGA. That year (1932), the PGA was match play (player against player) where he defeated Frank Walsh, 4 and 3, at the Keller Golf Club in St. Paul. Dutra played with the best players of that day, among them Craig Wood, Horton Smith, Paul Runyan, Gene Sarazen, Tommy Armour, and Walter Hagen.

My trip to Watsonville was worth it to meet this great person, a testament to the quality of golfers from the Monterey Peninsula.

Monterey Peninsula Herald   Friday, Jan. 14, 1972.

EXCLUSIVE
RADIO COVERAGE of the 'CROSBY'
KRML-1410
on your AM Dial
2, 15- MINUTE LIVE SHOWS EVERY HOUR
STARTING AT 9:00 A.M.
THURS.   FRI.   SAT.   SUN.
with Sportscasters
Johnny Lamb   Bob Murphy
Earle Russell
...direct from the play-action at
Pebble Beach, Cypress & Spyglass
Remember to tune to
KRML-1410
for all the 'CROSBY' action!

This is the ad we ran for KRML in the *Monterey Herald* to promote our coverage of the Bing Crosby Pro-Am in January, 1972.

One of the most popular golf tournaments on the tour has been the Bing Crosby Pro-Am held at Pebble Beach, Cypress Point, and Spyglass Hill. It was one tournament the pros looked forward to, and were anxious to play in because it was not only great tournament - it was a time to let your hair down and have some fun.

Bing always invited his best friends from Hollywood and the business world. They enjoyed coming to the Peninsula for great golf on spectacular courses, a chance to win some money, and to party a little. The Hollywood crowd included Guy Madison, Tom Harmon, Phil Harris, Jack Lemmon, George Scott, Jim Garner, and many more.

The pro contingent included Ken Venturi, Tony Lema, Jimmy Dameret, Gene Littler, Dave Stockton, George Archer, Don January, Byron Nelson, Ben Hogan, Cary Middlecoff, and other top touring pros who loved Bing and enjoyed this great Pro-Am. Jack Nicklaus always revered Pebble Beach and mentioned that if he had one more round of golf to play in his life, he would select Pebble Beach. Lee Trevino loved the courses but was never crazy about the weather which could be great, or simply horrible...rain, wind, cold, etc. Some golfers didn't like the Pro-Am concept where they were teamed with amateurs who weren't good sticks! (That means they weren't good golfers.)

Local business people looked forward to the Crosby because it was held at a time when the economy was at its lowest peak - January, or the first week in February. The Pro-Am was a boom for their cash registers.

After Bing Crosby passed away, the tournament took on the name of the AT&T National Pro-Am and has continued in the same format. It is held each year at the latter part of January, or the first week of February.

Cypress Point is no longer part of the venue, having backed out when the USGA (United States Golf Association) demanded that they had to include a minority as a member (African-American) to their club. At this writing, the new Shore Course at the Monterey Peninsula Country Club has replaced Cypress Point.

Jack Lemon

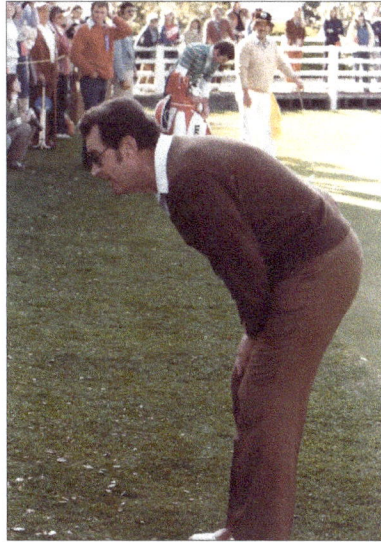

James Garner

Johnny Miller

George C. Scott

Art Wall, Jr.

Tom Watson

Jack Nicklaus

Telly Savalas

Johnny Mathis

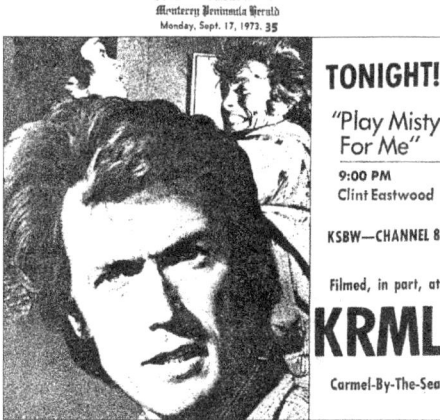

Unless you are from another planet or too young to remember, all movie fans and Clint Eastwood devotees know about *Play Misty For Me*, the movie filmed on the Monterey Peninsula in 1971. Many scenes were filmed at the KRML studios.

The history of the film is as follows: When Eastwood purchased the Hog's Breath Inn in Carmel, his partners were Walter Becker (who owned the Marquis Restaurant), and Paul Lippman, a writer from Montana who wrote for a San Francisco newspaper before coming to Carmel.

Lippman and I became friends, and for a period, he conducted a radio show on KRML, which I owned. He mentioned to me that Clint was going to make a film about a disc jockey who was being harassed by some wacko woman. Paul asked if I was interested in renting out our studios when we were off the air, and I agreed, not for the money but more for the publicity value, both national and international.

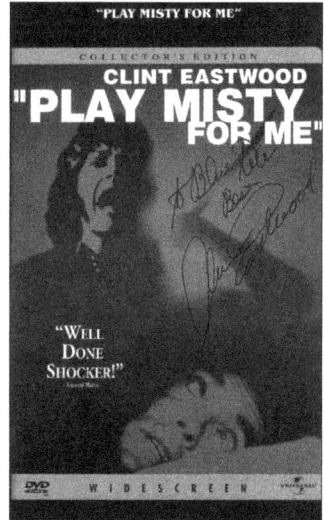

I signed the deal with Robert Daley, who at the time was Clint's representative on movie deals. (I still have a copy of the original contract signed by Daley for The Malpaso Company to rent KRML.) The crew would film from sunset to sunrise. It worked ideally because KRML was classified as a daytime station, sunrise to sunset.

The film crew worked 'til 6 a.m., just before I appeared to begin the *Sam The Morning Man* show.

Misty became a classic, and to this day is seen on a regular basis on the major TV networks when they play old films.

Paul Lippman severed his business relationship with Clint and Walter at the Hog's Breath Inn and moved to Palm Springs where he did some writing and got involved in promoting polo tournaments.

LAS VEGAS SUN—**19**
Thursday, November 4, 1971

Eastwood Portrays DeeJay

Clint Eastwood departs from his rugged outdoor roles to play a radio disc jockey in the Universal-Malpaso Company picture in Technicolor, "Play Misty For Me," which is now playing at the Cinerama Theatre.

During the location filming of the chilling suspense drama at Carmel, California's station KRML, the tall, rangy star was photographed at the turntables by a San Francisco newspaper.

The day after the photo was printed, deejays throughout the area began to get requests to play "Misty" and the Erroll Garner composition became a hit record all over again.

Co-starring with Eastwood in the film in which he directed, are Jessica Walter, Donna Mills and John Larch.

AT THE CINERAMA—"Play Misty For Me," which is now playing at the Cinerama Theatre, is a Universal-Malpaso Company picture in technicolor. It stars Clint Eastwood and Jessica Walter and is rated R—under 17 requires accompanying parent or adult guardian.

During my broadcast years at the Bing Crosby Pro-Am, I worked with the likes of Johnny Lamb, Bob Murphy, Bud Orlebeck of the *Monterey Herald*, and Bill Houle. The most unusual voice man was a local attorney and not an announcer. For the 1976 Crosby, I invited Jack Arancio, a Monterey attorney and a good golfer, to be part of our broadcasts. My rationale was that we needed some local color from one who had played these courses and could speak authoritatively, and that man was Arancio. He was also a member of the Monterey Peninsula Country Club.

Arancio was a good mix with the other broadcasters who were stationed at Cypress Point, Spyglass Hill, and Pebble Beach. I could relate to Arancio because we both played the courses before - he more than I, because at the time I was trying to grow KRML, through sales and a good music format.

Jack and I tried to outdo each other in the humor department during the radio reports and in between shows. I guess he had to use some humor in his legal dealings with clients, perhaps, or to entice judges for a decision in his favor.

When we were broadcasting our favorite line was: "Back to you, Jack!" In turn, he would emote, "Back to you, Sam!"

The years have gone by since those broadcast years, and even though it was a one shot deal between us, we have remained friends. I think he's retired as a lawyer and doesn't play golf anymore. When we do meet at certain social functions on the Monterey Peninsula, he'll say, "Back to you, Sam!" to which I'll reply, "Back to you, Jack!"

BROADCAST CHANGES, ALL ABOUT MONEY

What happened in 1972 regarding broadcasting rights, would never happen today. The rules were lax in those days; today, it's all about money and who has the most to pay for the privilege of broadcasting certain sporting events.

In 1972, for a small stipend to the USGA, KRML in Carmel received the broadcasts rights to cover the U.S. Open at Pebble Beach. It's hard to imagine such a grant even though the television rights went to one of the major TV networks.

The most surprising grant to our wish was the USGA allowing us to be right behind the 18th green with a broadcast stand, ideally positioned for us to see the entire 18th fairway and green. Today, this would never happen; you would be given a booth or seat in the press room away from all the action.

Johnny Lamb, who was on local television (KMST) at the time, worked with us because he had an in with Dan Searle and the Crosby committee, who worked in tandem with the USGA officials. That helped to pull off the deal! Unlike the Crosby, only one course was used in the Open – Pebble Beach – as opposed to the Crosby, which featured Pebble Beach, Cypress Point, and Spyglass Hill.

The highlight of the '72 Open, won by Jack Nicklaus, was his one-iron on the par three 17th hole. His shot hit the pin and landed just a few inches from the hole for a tap-in birdie.

One doesn't have to look hard to find out what caused radio and television rights to change; money does the talking. A case in point is TV coverage of the PGA Tour, which was in the hands of NBC, particularly the U.S. Open. The new television rights have been given to Fox. Again, money more than content and substance became the big factor in the decision. Johnny Miller and Dan Hicks, the golf casters for NBC, were not happy with the move, but that's the nature of the business! Money talks.

During the '60's on the Monterey Peninsula it was my job at the radio station to call on accounts and to help increase the revenue of the station. Without advertising, radio stations cannot exist; of course the same is true with all media, from newspapers to magazines, and television stations.

I encountered one fellow during my sales efforts who was a real character, to say the least. His name was Carl Nelson, and he was the owner of a used car lot who loved to ham it up on radio and television. Whatever the commercials, he would end it with, "I'm the king!"

We recorded most of the spots, as they are called, at the radio station, but there were times when we hauled a tape recorder to his office and turned him loose. He would love to expound about a certain car, and when he got through, even I was interested in purchasing the automobile.

"He's the king" became his slogan, and regardless of where he traveled on the Peninsula and in Salinas, he was recognizable to all from his many radio and television spots. If there was a rodeo in the area, he'd wear Western garb, and for other events he would dress accordingly. He made sure he was hip to the happenings of the day, thus his success.

Later when he sold his auto lot, Carl moved to the Central Valley, near Fresno, purchased a ranch, raised cattle, and grew some crops. He became a real cowboy, being the ham he was, and also did some bit parts for some motion pictures film in this area.

Carl befriended both Johnny Adams, my former program director at KRML, and me, and the relationship was a good one. Before he passed away, he sent some pictures taken by the studio during the filming of *Play Misty For Me* and wanted John or me to get Clint Eastwood to autograph one of these originals from the film. His demise came before we could get them signed.

Carl was a one-of-a-kind friend.

Johnny Lamb, the sports guy at KMST television in the early '70's had too much on his plate and was giving up the position.

Stoddard Johnson and Bill Schuyler, the owners of KMST-TV, approached me to handle the sports on the 6 p.m. and 11 p.m. broadcasts. It was a challenge for me, because I was still running KRML in Carmel, and that was my primary concern. It was a tough time raising children and trying to make a success at a radio station that never made money, regardless of who the owners were prior to my purchase. But Stoddard and Bill knew I liked sports and could convey a message to the viewers.

The problem with KMST is that it had only one camera, black and white with the camera switching from the newsman and then on to the sportscaster. The newscaster was Jim Dooley. One time the camera was on me and switched to him, and he was eating a banana. We did have our laughs.

When Jeff Richmond and Dana Kennedy (a real looker) came to work, the set changed and the viewing public got to hear two real professionals. Between 6 and 11 p.m., I journeyed over the Carmel Hill to my home in Carmel Knolls, ate and rested, only to go back over the hill for the next broadcast.

The exposure it gave me was enormous, because, unlike radio, the folks can see you and relate in a different manner as opposed to hearing one's voice and building a mental picture of the announcer.

I left the job after a few years and continued with my primary job as owner-manager of KRML in Carmel.

The fellow to the right of U.S. Open winner, Francis Ouimet, is Ed Lowery, excellent golfer and owner of Beattie Ford, Monterey!

I met a lot of interesting people while I was owner of KRML from 1968 to 1977. As a station owner I devoted a goodly portion of my work day in radio sales, calling on accounts on the Monterey Peninsula.

One of my accounts was Beattie Ford, located at Franklin and Washington Streets in downtown Monterey. Beattie's owner was Ed Lowery, a member of the Cypress Point Golf Club. Ed became popular as a youngster when he caddied for Francis Quimet when he won the U.S. Open at Brookline, Massachusetts. You probably have seen the picture of the little boy toting the golf bag for this large person who happened to be Quimet.

Mr. Lowery previously owned an auto agency in San Francisco. Ken Venturi and Harvie Ward worked as car salesmen when they weren't displaying their golf talents in amateur circles. Venturi and Ward, at the time, were the best amateurs in the world.

The book *The Match*, inspired by Mr. Lowery, was about these two amateurs taking on Ben Hogan and Byron Nelson at the Cypress Point Golf Course. The match took place long after the incident I'm writing about.

Mr. Lowery ushered me into his office and informed me that he wanted me to write a press release for the Italian golfer, Roberto Bernadini, who he was going to sponsor on the PGA tour. He gave me the particulars, and I wrote a press release highlighting the exploits of Mr. Bernadini.

A couple of days later I went to Mr. Lowery's office for approval of the press release. Though he hadn't read the release, he informed me that Mr. Bernadini was not coming to the States. He gave me no reason and didn't question the move. He turned to his secretary and said, "Cut Sam a check for $1000!" Mind you, this was in the '70's, and today that thousand dollars would be worth four times the amount.

Mr. Lowery was a generous person not only to me, but to everyone whose life he touched.

In the early 70's Clint Eastwood hosted a three-day tennis tournament at the Beach and Tennis Club at Pebble Beach with many tennis-playing Hollywood celebrities invited.

The event was broadcast on KRML with Johnny Adams, Lavonne Rae Andrews, and yours truly calling the action with a goodly amount of interviews.

Doug McClure, Jack Ging, Eddie LaBaron, Ross Martin, Jonathan Winters, James Franciscus, George Peppard, Greer Garson, and many others, including Big C (Clint) and Maggie Eastwood participated.

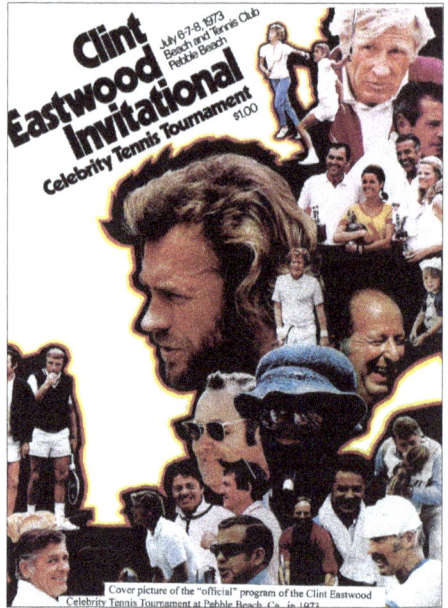

Cover picture of the "official" program of the Clint Eastwood Celebrity Tennis Tournament at Pebble Beach, Ca. in 1973.

Clint Eastwood Invitational Celebrity Tennis Tournament July 3rd 4th and 5th 1971 Pebble Beach $1.00

To Benefit Behavioral Sciences Institute Monterey

It was a time for fun and frivolity at the tournament and afterwards at the Hog's Breath Inn in Carmel, owned by Eastwood at the time.

Ken Green and Paul Lippman were part of Clint's committee which also included Don Hamilton who was the tennis pro at the Beach and Tennis Club.

The top entertainers were brought in for the event; the Sounds of Joy, and Page Cavanaugh, without the trio but with a band. All were there for the Saturday night gala.

The Pebble Beach Company president and a worthy contributor, Al Gawthrop, welcomed the event with open arms. The tournament was a Who's Who of top celebrities. Putting their tennis game on line were Charleston Heston, Merv Griffen, John Wayne and his wife, Pilar, and football great

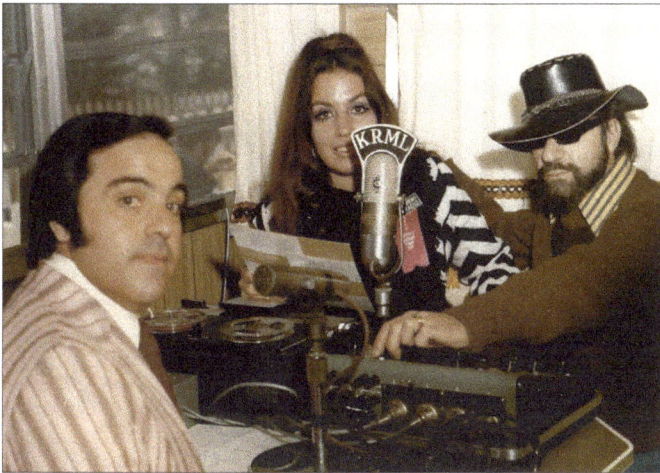

Matt Hazeltine. Bill Cosby added humor and a decent game, as did writer Herb Caen, who penned a column for a *San Francisco Chronicle.* With all these celebs, he had a good deal of material for his daily column.

Claudine Longet shared a microphone with us, displaying her latest poster and signing a few for the spectators.

This truly was a great time on the Monterey Peninsula and a precursor for the events that take place today. Clint truly has always been an innovator, and the Celebrity Tennis Tournament proved his vision for the area.

Committees For The Eastwood

Left to right -- Peter Herb, Paul Lippman, Clint, Don Hamilton and Ken Green. They may look like a barbershop quartet in bad need of a barber, but they are the fellows who make this thing hum.

The committee members who ran the Clint Eastwood Celebrity Tennis Tournament, most of whom were good tennis players.

Here are "Big C" (what we called Clint), Johnny, and me at the big charity
tennis tournament at Pebble Beach. We were all young at the time.

1410 is KRML on your dial

SAM "THE MORNING MAN"
6 — 9 AM

NICK GEORGE
9 AM — 2 PM

JOHNNY ADAMS
2 — SUNDOWN

"the personality station"

CARMEL BY-THE-SEA, CALIF.

The first couple of years at KRML we tried to get a large radio audience playing what we thought was the most palatable music for the day, because other stations were rocking to satisfy the younger audience. Our format appealed to the 35 to 55 age group and above. That meant we had to spin the likes of Frank Sinatra, Perry Como, Bing Crosby, and all the vocal groups, including The Four Freshman, The Lancers, Ray Coniff Singers, The Hi Lo's, and The Lettermen. We felt this made for a good audience, and our sound was the best in the Monterey County area.

Our business setback was the fact that we were designated by the FCC as a Daytime Station, meaning we signed on at Sunrise, and signed off at Sunset. In December that meant going off the air at 5 p.m. It was a killer for us, because the audience, in most cases, is very fickle and will dial elsewhere if you are not on the air when they dial in.

We believed in advertising even as broadcasters, and we ran print ads in the *Carmel Pine Cone.* A caricature of yours truly, on the 6 to 9 a.m. segment, followed by Nick George (Sousa was his given name) from 9 a.m. to 2 p.m., and then to finish the day to sundown was Johnny Adams, who threw in a bit of jazz to supplement his disc jockey stint.

Our only competitor with a middle-of-the-road format was KIDD, and it was difficult to compete with their station being on the air later than ours, but we did the best we could under the circumstances.

Too bad there aren't many radio stations around the nation playing our kind of format. Nowadays, folks can download music from the Internet. It's really a different world today.

EMCEE FOR THE NIGHT

SEATED at head table with his wife was dinner chairman Bert Cutino (photo above). Chef of the Year Peter Selaya (left) with his trophy and master of ceremonies Sam Salerno (photo at right).

Local Chefs Choose Their Favorite

Peter Selaya was named Chef of the Year Monday evening at the fourth annual President's Ball of the Monterey Peninsula Chefs' Association. And Monday was proclaimed Peter Selaya day by Monterey Mayor Gerald Fry, one of the distinguished guests at the ball. Although Mr. Selaya is master of the kitchen at the Pine Inn, which is in Carmel, the Monterey Mayor said he was no less a citizen of Monterey because "We recog-

nize Carmel as a part of Monterey..."

Nearly 300 guests, mostly persons engaged in the Peninsula's restaurant industry or members of local gourmet groups, were present at the lively affair, held at the Del Monte Hyatt House. At the conclusion of the award ceremony a seven-course dinner was served, complemented by four wines, at tables centered with chef's toques filled with red and white flowers.

The main course was Medallions of "Delft Blue" Veal with sauce Calvados, the veal flown in from the Los Angeles area by executive jet especially for the dinner. Dessert was Dobosch torte, served from glowing glass containers borne to the dining room by marching white-clad waiters.

Host chef was Richard Maglietto of the Hyatt House, and the dinner committee

During the years I owned KRML in Carmel, I was called upon to be master of ceremonies for many events that took place on the Monterey Peninsula, from golf tournaments to speaking engagements for various organizations.

When I joined Kiwanis in Carmel and the members found out that I had worked in Las Vegas in the '50's and '60's, I was invited to speak about the foibles of Sin City and what made the town tick. I gave them all the information regarding its quick growth, what the demographics of the town consisted of (it was a town then), where the hotel workers came from, and how best to spend your money there. Also, what was in town to interest people other than gambling.

I usually began my oration regarding Las Vegas by telling folks how they can make a small fortune when they go to Sin City. The answer? Just arrive there with a large fortune! (*Drum roll*)

Another popular event on the Peninsula was the Rappa Golf Tournament, put on by Rappa's Restaurant on Wharf #1. Many sports celebrities were invited each year. I not only played in the event, but handled the emcee chores. Brothers Sal and Joe Rappa were heavily involved in all aspects of the tournament.

Each year a local chef was honored for his culinary arts, and again, I was asked to handle the introductions, etc. Bert Cutino of the Sardine Factory was instrumental in choosing me for the honors. Each year a different chef was chosen from the great restaurants, and each year a different venue was selected.

It was my pleasure to be chosen for these specials events.

44—S.F. EXAMINER   Tues. Feb. 13. 1979

Nelson Cullenward

Laughs on the links

Bob Hope, Bing Crosby ham it up on the course

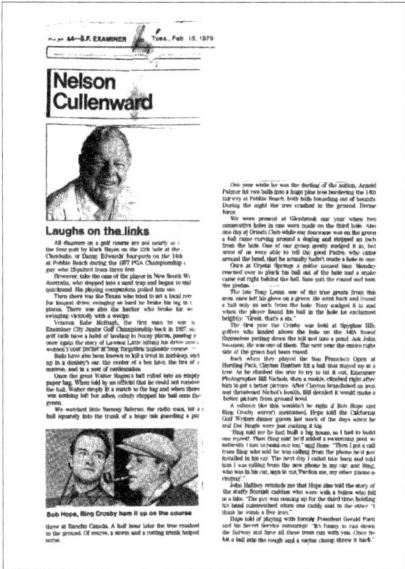

The year was 1979. I had the opportunity to be a participant in the Spalding Pro-Am, which was the brainstorm of Harold Firstman, a golf professional who (like his name) was first in new innovations. He was one of the first to combine professional women golfers, competing with the men. He invited men from the regular tour, LPGA stars, celebrities, and players on the lesser known tours.

In the tournament I played in, one of the courses used was Rancho Canada East at the mouth of Carmel Valley. One of the top golf writers in the Bay Area was Nelson Cullenward, a low handicapper and a lefty, to boot. In our group Larry Ziegler was our pro, and at the time, one of the best on the regular tour. Nelson was a jovial fellow and great to be around to talk sports, or to have a toddy for the body.

The day we played Rancho Cañada, the wind was kicking up a storm, so to speak, and unless you were a wind player, it was going to be a rough day. Not for the pros, but more for we amateurs who couldn't master all the shots needed in this kind of weather.

At the time, Rancho Cañada featured many trees on both courses, East and West. The third hole was a three par over the Carmel River, measuring at least 175 yards from the back tees. I reached the third tee and inquired to Ziegler as to what club I should use, even though I had a three wood in mind, and that's what Larry said to hit.

I swung as hard as I could,. At the time there was a large tree to the left of the green, and I caught it right in the center. The ball came back, and I chipped it close for a good three.

When we got to the sixth tee, we heard a loud crack, and the tree I hit came tumbling down. We had a few chuckles about the incident, and Nelson even gave it some ink in his daily column in the *San Francisco Examiner*.

When he came to town for coverage of sporting events, we reminisced about my power game.

BOBBY CLAMPETT

One of the best golfers to come from the Monterey Peninsula was Bobby Clampett. Bobby cut his teeth in golf at Quail Lodge and Country Club in Carmel Valley. He lived on the property at a condo with his mother, Jacqueline. He pounded balls for hours under the tutelage of Ben Doyle, who taught him the mechanics of the golf swing.

Clamplett won many junior tournaments while he attended Robert Louis Stevenson School at Pebble Beach. He also won the California Amateur Tournament held yearly at Pebble. When he attended Brigham Young University in Utah, he was considered one of the best collegiate golfers in the country. I've maintained that as a youngster he had more shots than any golfer; Tiger Woods comes closest to what I saw.

We became friends when I spoke to the Middle School students on the subject of broadcasting. At the time, I was owner and operator of KRML, just a few blocks from Middle School. During his years as an analyst for CBS, Bobby attributed his interest in broadcasting to KRML, which was nurtured by my speech to the students.

Clampett was destined for greatness until that hiccup in the 1982 British Open at Troon. He opened with a 66, followed with a 67 the second day, and then faltered with a 76 and 77 to allow Tom Watson to sneak in another Open victory.

Bobby and I played once at the Monterey Peninsula Country Club on the Dunes Course. During the round, he showed me some golf shots, even one in the kneeling position. I didn't try the shot. I think he scored a 69 and this golfer had an 82.

We've maintained our friendship and see each other on occasions when he visits his mom in Carmel, or if he plays in a tournament here.

One never knows what his career would resemble had he not faltered at Troon in 1982, although he did win after the Open experience.

THE GOLF CLINIC AT PEBBLE BEACH

In the early eighties, Harold Firstman asked if I was interested in handling the camera work for the Golf Clinic at Pebble Beach which he owned. Never having been an expert with cameras, I was a little hesitant at first, but after due consideration, I accepted the position. It was a television camera and not too complicated to operate. I perused the information regarding the camera one weekend and then was ready to go.

The Golf Clinic brought in folks desiring to improve their golf game, or those who were beginners to the sport. National advertising was done to entice the folks to come to Pebble Beach for lessons, or a tune-up for those who already knew the game. The participants stayed at the Lodge or at Spanish Bay at Pebble Beach and commenced all activities starting Monday with exercises (minimal amount), then proceeded to hit balls with instructors present. On certain segments, I was taking pictures of their swings as the instructor gave advice.

The lessons took place at the driving range at Spyglass Hill. Among the instructors were John Geertsen Senior and Junior, Dana Booth, formerly the pro at Spyglass Hill, Ed Oldfield (from Chicago) who at the time tutored many of the LPGA players, Dennis Rose, pro on the Big Island of Hawaii, and Claude Harmon, one of the top teaching pros in the world.

Working with me and a delightful assistant was Jeff Firstman, Harold's son, a good worker and fun to be around. The lessons would continue with the students playing nine holes at Spyglass Hill, and one day 18 holes at Pebble Beach. I would film them on the 1st hole, move the equipment to the 7th hole, and present them with the tape on Friday morning when their week was over. A group picture was taken and presented to each student.

During this period, I mentioned to Harold that I thought Pebble Beach would start their own clinic; they owned the courses, owned the hotels, and had their own pros to teach. Well, needless to say, they now have The Academy and a great facility it is.

I think Harold Firstman was an innovator, by virtue of his Spalding Invitational Golf Tournament, which featured top pros and top LPGA pros (this had never been done before) and his Golf Clinic at Pebble Beach. Nice to have smart people around these parts!

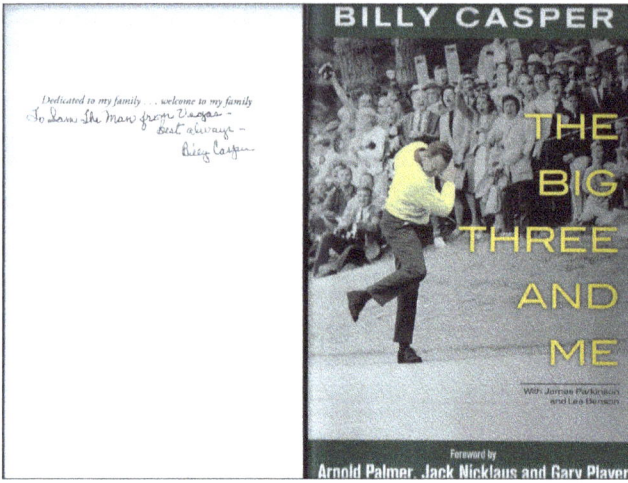

Underrated but one of the best in his era, Billy Casper was never given the proper recognition at a time when he truly earned it. But he was competing with the popularity of Arnold Palmer, Jack Nicklaus, and Gary Player.

From 1956 to 1971, Billy Casper won at least one tournament a year; that's 16 straight years, and quite a fete. He won a total of 51 tournaments, which ranks high among all touring pros.

Billy thinks he was slighted, and I tend to agree, mainly because he was a soft spoken person and wasn't looking for the spotlight. Because of his low-key demeanor, the press catered to Palmer, Nicklaus, and Player.

Casper was destined to be a great golfer, and the logistics really helped. The San Diego area where he grew up was conducive to producing great golfers, in the form of Gene Littler, and later, Phil Mickelson. It's no secret that California has produced a bevy of great golfers, to wit: Venturi, Lema, Archer, Clampett, Johnny Miller, Olin Dutra, Al Gieberger, and Craig Stadler, to name a few.

Five years ago, Casper published a book called *The Big Three and Me* and in it, he divulged his feeling about being shunned by the media and golf in general, even though his record at the time was the best of all players for a fifteen year period.

Since Billy converted to Mormonism, he has resided in Utah, raised a large family, and has been a good ambassador for golf, his family, and for his church.

It was a pleasure to spend some time with Casper, both in Las Vegas during the Tournament of Champions, and most recently when he was honored by the golf association for his accomplishments. He passed away in 2015.

When professional golfers are asked what they consider the best job in golf for a club pro, the answer is always Cypress Point Golf Course on the Monterey Peninsula. In the early Crosby days the highlight for any pro playing in the tournament was his practice round at Cypress and then to include that in the rotation of the tournament.

Having played the course many times with Clint Eastwood and others, it has been a definite plus to play these fabulous eighteen holes, for its picturesque beauty, its design, and most importantly, the pro who called the shots there for over 35 years, Jim Langley. Jim was not only a good golfer, but very personable and friendly with whomever he met.

Jim and the Langley family were close friends of mine who lived in Carmel Views when my family lived in Carmel Knolls, one hill over at the mouth of Carmel Valley. When I became a single parent raising my son Sam, the Langleys were there to be surrogate parents. But the Langleys were there for everyone when someone was in need. They were also active in the Catholic church at the Mission. Jim's son, Brett, was my son's closest friend, as they grew up in Carmel, and on many weekends they were inseparable.

I can truthfully say that in all the years I've lived on the Monterey Peninsula, I never heard a negative word about Jim, his wife, or family. They were truly the ideal American family.

I had the opportunity to play with Jim in the Spalding Invitational Golf Tournament, and one of the venues was at Laguna Seca Golf Ranch. Just before he retired, Jim allowed my son and me to play Cypress, and it was incredible, sharing the game with my son on a beautiful Monterey Peninsula day.

Jim passed away this past year, much attributed to the horrible car accident he was in a few years back, which caused him to lose the use of one arm.

One arm or not, Jim is hitting golf shots on the great course in the heavens. Truly, a great American!

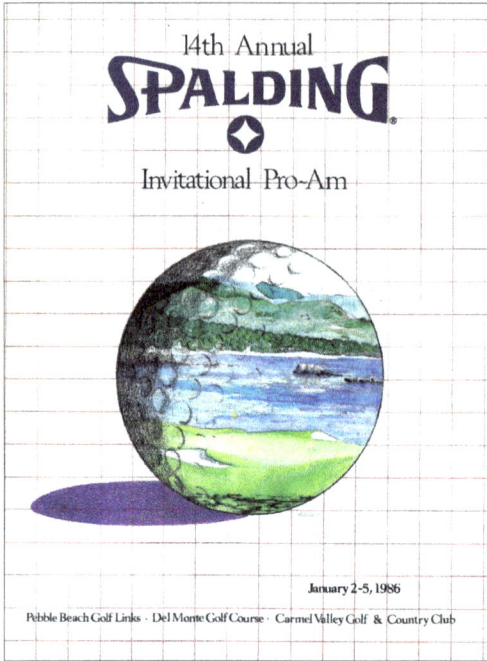

14th Annual
SPALDING
Invitational Pro-Am

January 2-5, 1986

Pebble Beach Golf Links · Del Monte Golf Course · Carmel Valley Golf & Country Club

It was never a problem getting a local artist to grace the cover of one of the magazines I produced, particularly the Spalding Pro-Am and the Crosby publications.

The deal I usually made with the artists was to have them produce a painting for the cover, and I would give them the exclusive. They in turn owned the original, would receive a picture story in the publication, and I would received the second numbered print. It was a win-win situation for both of us and never was any artist unhappy with the terms. No money exchanged hands.

The reason I mention this is I thought I would give my niece a shot at one of my publications, and she agreed. Her name was Jan Salerno, my brother Frank's daughter, who was a good graphic artist who did work for Donna Summers and other recording stars. Jan had gone to Brazil to elevate her education in art and graphics. My brother, Frank, a captain with United Airlines, made sure his daughter Jan got the right training to exploit her talents.

I gave Jan the idea of what I wanted on the cover of the 14th Annual Spalding Magazine: I told her I'd like to see the 18th green at Pebble Beach through a golf ball!

I was pretty ecstatic when I received her art work, because it was exactly the idea I conveyed to her. Of all the publications I've produced through the years this was one of the best and received a great deal of comment.

Nice to have talent in the family!

At this writing, Jan lives in Hawaii and continues her art and design work

It was a glorious time in the mid-eighties in Carmel, particularly when it was announced that Clint Eastwood was running for mayor of this sleepy community. Bud Allen, who at one time owned the La Playa hotel, was instrumental in selecting a worthy contender to the incumbent mayor. I was even approached for the role, but I'm no politician as I explained to Bud.

A few days later one of Bud's henchmen came to see me and told me, "Forget it, we have the man!" And when he informed me that Clint Eastwood was that man I said, "That's great, and I'll work with whomever on the campaign."

To tell you that everyone was ecstatic would be putting in mildly. Elinor Laiolo and Bob Fischer were running with Clint for the Council spots. It was kind of a troika with each on the same page. I was approached to work Fischer's campaign and I agreed to handle the chore. All of Clint's friends were set to go. We attended coffee sessions and meetings with groups promoting the threesome. It was a joyous time, with most locals on Clint's bandwagon.

There had been some rumors that Clint ran because the City of Carmel had turned him down on a plan for his building on San Carlos Street. The City Council had turned down a request for a six-inch variance on the roof at the back of a wonderful building designed by the renowned architect George Brook-Kothlow. The conversation was that Clint wanted to get even with the City, but that was a bunch of baloney. He didn't like the way Carmel was run, and he wanted to change things. His win brought

CLINT EASTWOOD FOR MAYOR

This is My Home

"People ask me: 'But do you have the time? Can you really be the Mayor?'

"I cannot promise the people of Carmel that I will never leave town in the next two years, but I have thought a lot about this job. I can control my time. I can promise the citizens that Carmel will be my first priority and I will spend whatever time it takes to be the best Mayor this city ever had.

"This is my home. This is where I have chosen to live. It is where my friends are, it is where my heart is. I am not asking you to elect me as Mayor in order to disappoint you.

"I am asking you to elect me as Mayor so that we can work together for a City we can be proud of, and for a quality of life that is unexcelled anywhere.

"Please give me your vote on April 8. I know you will not be disappointed."

CLINT EASTWOOD FOR MAYOR

PAID FOR BY FRIENDS OF CLINT EASTWOOD, P.O. BOX 4300, CARMEL, CA 93921

Paid Political Advertisement

Thank You ...

To all Carmel voters, negative or affirmative, I thank you for caring enough to vote. Special thanks to my campaign contributors and helpers, also to **Sam Salerno**, **Barbara Reed**, and to my wife, **Marian**.

Good wishes and congratulations to Clint and Elinor.

Carmel, I love you.

Bob Fischer

The Carmel
CAMPAIGN
SCRAPBOOK

$5.00

SPECIAL COMMEMORATIVE 1st EDITION

Clint Eastwood:
Mayor of Carmel-by-the-Sea

vast revenues to the Carmel business community, and filled out his two-year term. No negativity ever marred his time in office.

I was happy to be part of the campaign, and I remain friends with all those who participated. At this writing, Bob Fischer is no longer with us. He served his time as a policeman and councilman with honor for the City of Carmel-by-the-Sea.

C L I N T   E A S T W O O D

April 6, 1988

Dear Neighbor:

Next week, Tuesday, April 12, we go to the polls
to elect a new mayor and two council members. I am appealing
for your support, as I did two years ago, to help continue
the progress that has been started in solving many of Carmel's
persistent problems.

I think the candidates who have worked the hardest
on behalf of the city and would work the hardest in the future
are Jean Grace for Mayor and Carla Ramsey and Howard Neiman,
Jr. for council members. After two years of results, it's
very important that we don't return to the old ways of
distrust, bad humor and no action.

It's just as important this time as last time that
you be sure to vote on Tuesday. When you do, it will mean
a lot to the future of Carmel if you vote for Jean Grace,
Carla Ramsey and Howard Neiman, Jr.

Thank you for your consideration.

Best,

Clint Eastwood

Clint Eastwood at the Hog's Breath Inn, with me looking on.
Clint's tee shirt is not as fancy as mine!

A ROUND OF GOLF WITH CLINT EASTWOOD

After Clint Eastwood filmed "Play Misty For Me" at KRML, the station I owned at the time, we became good friends and played quite a bit of golf together, with friends Steve King, Phil Dacey, and Jim Freeman. Freeman was a retired Naval officer with a degree from the Naval Academy at Annapolis. He played football and was a teammate of Roger Staubach.

Clint was a member of the exclusive Cypress Point Golf Course at Pebble Beach and he was generous always to invite us to share the links with him.

I can remember one afternoon at Cypress Point when the wind was howling and Clint had hit a shot behind a tree. It was a dangerous second shot but he took the gamble and went for it. Well, the ball hit the tree and came back and almost nailed him. What a scare. But it didn't stop there.

On another long four par, I was about to hit a three wood and didn't realize that Clint was in my line of fire. I hit the shot (the wind still howling) and it was headed right for Clint. I yelled fore but with the wind blowing so furiously, he didn't hear my shout. Luckily the ball didn't hit him. That was quite an experience. On two occasions that day, we could have lost the GREATEST movie icon ever!

By the way, Eastwood does not call me by my name but calls me Blue Tees, which are placed the further distance from the hole, because he always wanted to play the regular tees which were a bit closer. Today, if I play the ladies tees, the closest to the green, I'm satisfied.

Phil Dacey, who was part of our group, is no longer with us. Jim Freeman makes his home in Texas. Steve King and I still play golf together and see Clint on occasion.

MEN'S SCORE CARD — CYPRESS POINT CLUB

HOLE	BLUE TEES RATED 72.5	WHITE TEES RATED 71.0	PAR	HANDICAP STROKES	SAM / PHIL	STEVE / CLINT
1	418	408	4	5	5 6	4 5
2	551	538	5	1	5 7	5 6
3	161	156	3	17	4 4	3 4
4	385	377	4	7	4 6	5 5
5	491	478	5	11	6 7	5 6
6	522	511	5	3	5 5	6 5
7	163	159	3	15	5 3	3 4
8	355	334	4	9	6 4	4 6
9	291	286	4	13	4 5	4 4
Total Out	3337	3247	37		43 47	39 45

HOLE	BLUE TEES RATED 72.5	WHITE TEES RATED 71.0	PAR	HANDICAP STROKES	SAM PHIL STEVE CLINT
10	491	480	5	16	5 6 5 6
11	434	423	4	4	5 5 4 4
12	409	400	4	2	6 3 5 6
13	362	339	4	14	5 4 5 5
14	383	378	4	8	5 6 6 5
15	139	124	3	18	3 4 4 3
16	233	218	3	6	4 4 4 5
17	376	364	4	10	5 5 5 6
18	342	327	4	12	5 5 5 4
Total In	3169	3053	35		
Total Out	3337	3247	37		
Total	6506	6300	72		

Scorer: SAM SALERNO

Attest: _(signature)_

Date: SEPTEMBER 1, 1985

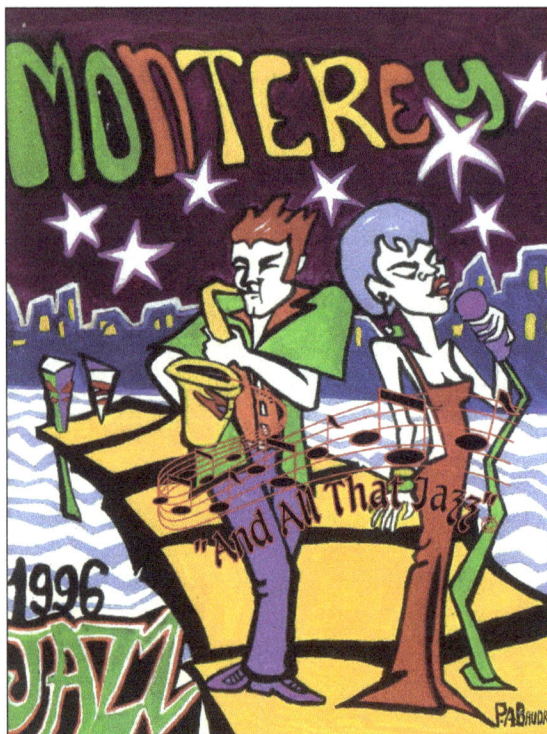

Along with my love for broadcasting, I've had an affinity for publishing because of my writing experience.

As I have noted, I have published many magazines, tabloids, and posters. A couple of the magazines were inspired by my friend and co-hort, Johnny Adams. He's been on the jazz scene on the Monterey Peninsula longer than most people live, and he knows so much about the music he has played for years on local radio stations.

We put our heads together about publishing a jazz magazine during the Monterey Jazz Festival week, not to compete with the other publications, mind you, but to give the locals a different take on the event. We were smart enough to disclaim our production, and urged those who read our magazine to purchase the official magazine.

Instead of the Festival committee embracing our publication, they decided to sue us for so-called copyright infringement. The suit was dropped, but it did cost me some money to hire attorneys to answer their suit. Johnny and I were at a loss, and to this day wonder why it happened. After all, what were we promoting, the Newport Jazz Festival? No, we were promoting the Monterey Jazz Festival, not Johnny's or Sam's Festival! That's life.

EDITORIAL

What ever happened to the free enterprise system in America? And first amendment rights? .... which reads in the Constitution of the United States: "Congress shall make no laws respecting an establishment of religion, or prohibiting the free exercise thereof; or abridging the freedom of speech, or of the press; or the right of the people to peaceably assemble, and to petition for a redress of grievances." Weren't these the laws and attributes that made America the global power and leader it is today?

Apparently, the entrepreneurs who run the Monterey Jazz Festival have forgotten these principles or how they themselves became successful....it's called FREE ENTERPRISE! The idea of squelching or shutting out two individuals whose names and backgrounds are synonymous with JAZZ in this area is preposterous and illegal!

Again this year, the Monterey Jazz Festival ignored the first amendment rights of individuals by sending out a letter to each sponsor who appeared in our publication of last year. They tried to discredit our magazine and integrity by viciously attacking our character and honesty by labeling our publication "bogus" and urging clients to buy an ad in the "official" magazine and not ours; and if they did, they would receive a discount.

My partner, Johnny Adams, and I have been associated with "JAZZ" long before the Monterey Jazz Festival was an embryo, dating from the early 1950's. As broadcasters, we played jazz music on radio, conducted jazz interviews with recording stars, and promoted "jazz" concerts in the area; so we are no novices in this department. My partner has remained in jazz as an announcer and "jazz writer," while I ventured into management and radio station ownership and was formerly owner of KRML in Carmel. In addition to broadcasting, I found a love in the print medium and have published some 30 magazines.

Ever since we ventured into production of a jazz magazine, which we distribute "free" during the festival, we have been harassed and even sued by the Monterey Jazz Festival. The suit, which took place at the time of our first publication in 1982, was dropped because we agreed not to use their "logo" and to adhere to certain distribution areas. Their actions this year are grounds for a tremendous libel suit, but my partner and I are too busy promoting jazz and putting out the "best" and most authoritative magazine possible this year, and every year that the festival exists.

Why haven't they harassed the Herald, Pine Cone, television and radio stations who promote the same event in this market? Remember, it's "free enterprise." When an event takes place on the Monterey Peninsula, be it the AT&T, Laguna Seca Races, Bach Festival, etc., media (and we're part of the media) can exploit the event.

We did hire an attorney to send a message for them to "cease and desist." They obliged, but the damage was done, they thought. Much to their chagrin, it didn't work, and will not work, because we have "paid our dues in this market." If the committee would stop and reflect, who are we promoting? Ourselves? We don't need the promotion . . . our backgrounds and credibility speak for themselves. And why so much animosity toward my partner, Johnny Adams? There were times as a fourth estater he was denied Press credentials. If the committee has a beef with him, sit down with him and explain the problems. Isn't that the American way? Put the cards on the table.

It is our conclusion that the members responsible for these actions should take their energies and apply them to a positive situation; and thank our forefathers who made laws so that we could be free and enjoy the fruits of our labor. And to enjoy JAZZ! Remember, thus far, it's a free country!

Sam Salerno

I was lured to golf interviews because of my love for the game and the fact that I had access to such sports celebrities by virtue of being a broadcaster. Besides sports coverage, at small market radio stations, one had to read cold news, spin records, handle interviews with local politicians, etc. If you were lucky as I was, you covered sporting events.

In Fort Bragg, California, I broadcast my first football game played in Fortuna between the Fort Bragg High School team and Fortuna's team. I was a green horn but that's how one got experience.

Jack Nicklaus at Pebble Beach

I began covering golf events in Las Vegas during the Tournament of Champions, which was played at the Desert Inn Country Club behind the Desert Inn Hotel. It was a good experience, and what made it somewhat easy was the attitude of the pro golfers themselves. Never did they turn down interviews regardless of your stature in broadcasting. Palmer, Nicklaus, Player, and the rest were very friendly and cooperative with the press. One can't say that about most sports figures today.

In addition to the Tournament of Champions I gained more knowledge with reports from the Sahara Invitational, which was played at the Stardust Golf Course in Las Vegas, and years of reporting at the Bing Crosby Pro-Am and the AT&T Pro-Am, played on the Monterey Peninsula.

I can sympathize with many sports celebrities who turn down certain reporters who don't know the subject matter. I must admit, there are many who are uninformed who make fools of themselves because they don't do their homework.

From Bing Crosby, Byron Nelson and Olin Dutra, to Arnold Palmer, Ken Venturi, Gene Littler, Don January, Julius Boros, and Jerry Barber, I've done interviews with all of them. It's been a great run!

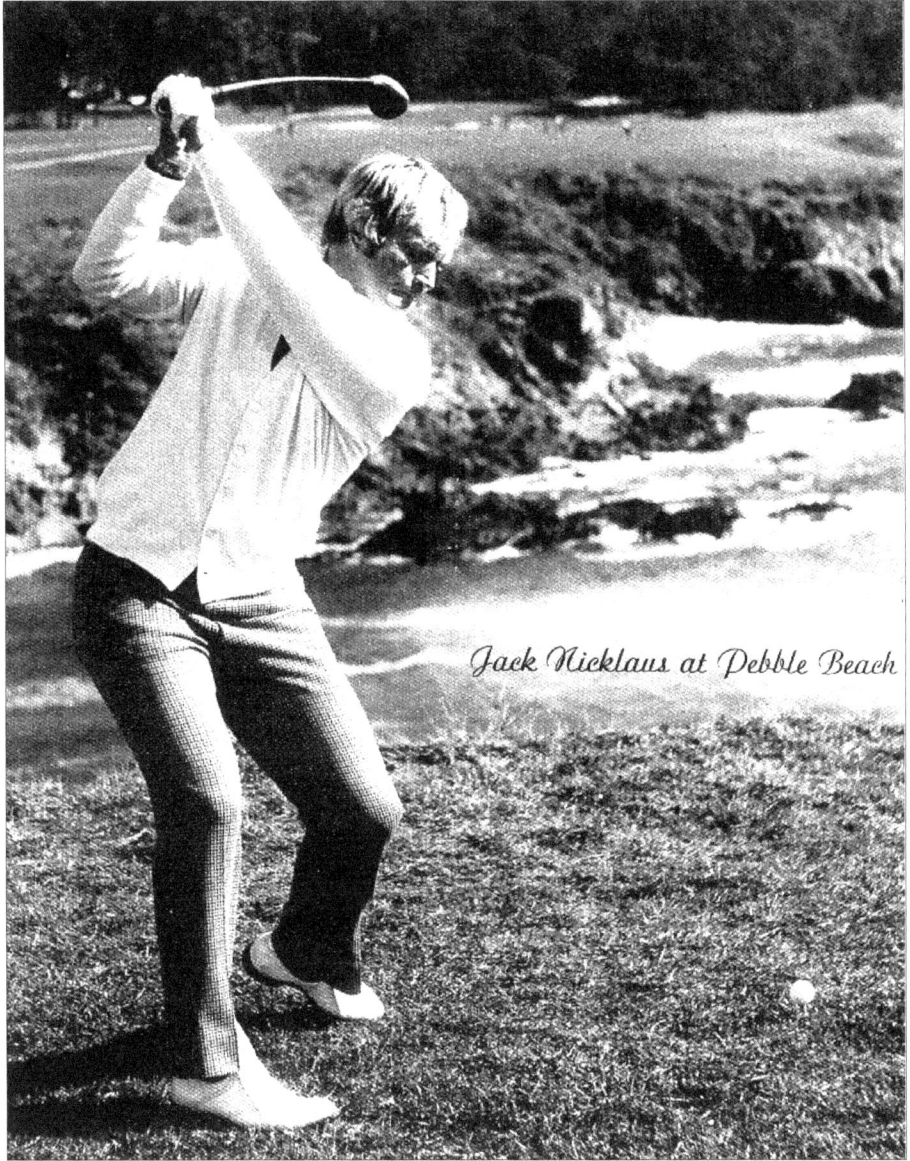

Jack Nicklaus at Pebble Beach

Jack Nicklaus tees it up at Pebble Beach. Jack says it is his favorite golf course.

I first met the man when he was selling insurance on the Monterey Peninsula. The meeting took place at what was then known as Sambo's, an eatery at the mouth of Carmel Valley. His name was Jerry Douglas, and when he wasn't selling insurance, he was flying to Los Angeles to record national television commercials, which helped to supplement his income.

Douglas had a great voice for commercials and also was no novice in the acting department. Johnny Adams, my program director at KRML, introduced me to Jerry, and with Steve King, another buddy, we played a bit of golf when the time permitted.

Jerry knew his time was limited on the Monterey Peninsula if he was going to break into Hollywood and make good with his talents. Carmel and the rest of the contiguous cities are fine, but not for making the big dough as an actor and becoming recognized nationally.

During one of his trips south, he got himself a great agent and manager, and the rest is history. He became a regular on *The Young and the Restless*, which has lasted for over thirty years.

When Johnny Adams and I traveled to Palm Springs, we spent two days at Jerry's guest house in Studio City. He showed us all the in hot spots in Beverly Hills and we had a good time.

In addition to his acting stint, Jerry appears at various nightclub venues, either as a soloist or with the group from the *Young and the Restless*. He has a powerful voice and he's a good entertainer, singing and telling jokes.

Remember, when you watch *The Young and the Restless* to look for the dashing Mr. Abbot, the part Jerry plays. Remember also, that he was once selling insurance before he became famous. If you're ambitious, there's always hope.

The Italians are not known for their golfing prowess; they're really just finding out what the game is all about. It's really not their sport if you compare it to football (soccer) or bocce.

What I'm about to expose to humanity is another form of golf played by four gentlemen who have Italian roots. They are Americans whose parents and relatives emigrated from Italy.

Bob DeLuca was from Boston and was living in Carmel, a grad from Boston University whose major was communications. While in the service in the Far East, he wrote for *Stars & Stripes*. When we first became friends, Bob was selling ophthalmology equipment for one of the large companies.

Jack Arancio was a Monterey attorney who loved golf and could tell a yarn or two.

Ernie Bennetti was from San Francisco and a close friend of Ken Venturi. Ernie was jack-of-all-trades and when we first met, he was selling real estate. Later, he became a bartender and golf marshal for the Pebble Beach Company.

I'm the fourth party of this group. Our similarities were unique; we all had a moustache, and if you didn't know it and saw us in person, we could pass for brothers, though we are all from diversified backgrounds. Our parents and relatives came from different parts of Italy and Sicily. We were paisanos, and we all loved golf.

We decided to conduct the first Italian Open with just four players. Prior to the game we met at The Forge In The Forest in Carmel, a bar/restaurant and an in spot at the time. While we were there, it began to rain heavily. It continued for hours, hindering our thoughts of ever playing golf. We all decided that we would call this The First Italian Open. By the time the rain stopped, we were in no condition to play.

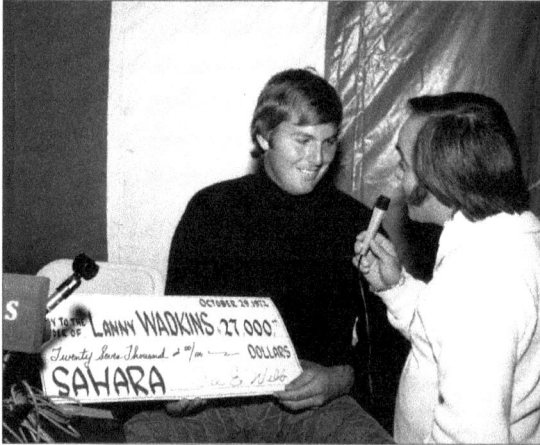

In the early 80's, Bob Logefeil, a golfing buddy and I came up with the idea that the Monterey Peninsula needed a publication that covered both golf and tennis. The result was the magazine *Golf & Tennis West*. It wasn't the regular magazine size, 8½ by 11, but somewhat smaller.

Of course the success of the magazine was predicated on the amount of ads sold and the reception from the local populace. We had some good writers in the form of Andy Briant, the tennis pro at the Beach and Tennis Club, John Powers, the golf coach at the Stevenson School at Pebble Beach, Mary Rodriguez, and Bob Logefeil.

The covers of our publications included Nancy Lopez, the top golfer on the LPGA Tour at that time, Lee Trevino at the tail end of his career, and Wimbledon Champion Bjorn Borg.

Our idea was to promote the magazine and get the revenues up to a point where we could sell the magazine, but that never worked out. Like the old proverb, he who makes no mistakes, makes nothing!

We lasted about a year and then went dark because Bob became a representative for a golf company in Southern California. We remained friends, and I realized that he had to go where the job paid more.

Logefeil moved to Park City, Utah. In addition to golf, he was an excellent skier and even taught the sport.

So much for a good idea. Perhaps one day in the future we may revive *Golf & Tennis West*.

AND ALL THAT JAZZ

The meeting took place in the early '50's when I was announcing a nightly live show from the San Carlos Hotel in Monterey. I had just completed my broadcast with Jose Flores and his Pan-American Trio when I was stopped by a fellow who apparently was impressed with the broadcast. He had a well-modulated voice and mentioned that he'd like to get into broadcasting.

His name at the time was Ettore Maffezzoli. Not your normal radio name, but at that juncture, I was only interested in his aspirations and desires.

I gave Ettore (he was called Tony) all the information regarding the School of Radio Arts I attended in Hollywood. When he arrived in Hollywood, Bill Ogden, one of the main instructors at the school, branched off and started a radio operations course in Burbank, and that's where Ettore went to learn about every facet of broadcasting, including elocution, music appreciation, script writing, etc.

A year and a half later, Ettore received his graduation papers, and he was off and running. We met again in Monterey, and the first thing I said to Ettore was, "Your new name is Johnny Adams." This name has been with him longer than his given name. Johnny worked for KIDD, KDON, and KRML when I owned it. He was never one to enjoy reading the news; his one love was jazz, and he interspersed it with our middle-of-the-road format. He was totally immersed in jazz music, jazz musicians, and jazz vocalists, many whom he knew and interviewed through the years.

Johnny/Tony/Ettore also worked for me in Las Vegas when I was program director of KRAM in the Flamingo Hotel. He later became my program director at KRML. His friendship with Clint Eastwood gave him a one-line speaking part as a bartender in the film *Bird*, which depicted the life of jazz great Charlie Parker. Johnny passed away in November of 2014, leaving many great memories of the wonderful radio shows he produced. All the local old-time radio broadcasters are leaving the scene; first Ed Dickinson (2014) and now Johnny Adams. We hope the area produces some new music men.

Book Review • "Harry Love"

by Sam Salerno

11/6/03

This historical novel is replete with excitement, a book which is difficult to put down because of its continuity and interest. It moves with the speed of the horsemen depicted in the book.

Harry Love, and his deputized Rangers traveled all the trails of early California during the Gold Rush, circa 1850, trying to capture the elusive Joaquin Murrieta and his group of Mexican banditos who pillaged all the gold mining towns of California. They stole money and gold in their reign of terror to glorify Mexico and killed anyone who resisted their demands. On occasion, Chinese workers (who also panned for gold) were hanged because the banditos didn't like their ponytails.

Paul Lippman has researched the period to the hilt, with nuances and verbiage that only one who lived during that era could expound. If you lack a history knowledge of California during the Gold Rush days, "Harry Love" will enlighten you to what you've missed with visits to cities, towns, rivers, and scenery of early California.

Harry Love, a Mexican War hero, had 90 days, with his Ranger company of 21, to capture or kill Joaquin Murrieta. I'm sure that "Harry Love" will be made into a Hollywood film because it is filled with action, adventure, and characters synonymous with the times and growth of California. Lippman didn't forget to whet the reader's sexual appetite, offering a hot and torrid chapter that'll have your blood boiling….a great segue from the norm.

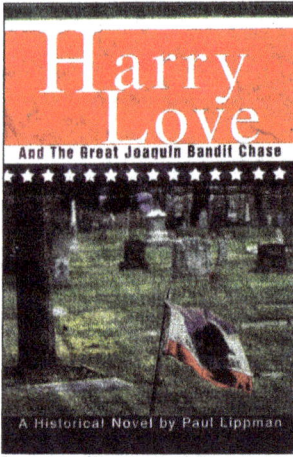

If you love adventure, intrigue, and suspense, "Harry Love" makes for sensational reading. It's a "must" on your reading list. Lippman can now be categorized as one of America's great writers. I'm happy to say I know him!

I have mentioned Paul Lippman in previous chapters and the fact that he was one of the original partners in the Hog's Breath Inn in Carmel with Clint Eastwood and Walter Becker.

Paul Lippman was a friend during his time in Carmel and remained a friend after he left the area. First and foremost, he was a brilliant writer, and we can attest to that fact by what he wrote in some of my golf magazines. He was kind enough to jot some words for me when I needed a real pro. Before we met, he was a writer for the *San Francisco Examiner.*

During his time away from Carmel, he spent time in Los Angeles and Palm Springs doing public relations and putting on polo matches. He was always one to cater to the social class as he did as part of Clint's committee during Clint's Invitational Celebrity Tennis Tournament held in 1973.

I knew Paul had a book in his DNA and was I surprised when I received his literary work, *Harry Love and the Great Joaquin Bandit Chase,* the story of a California sheriff and his posse on the hunt for the great Joaquin Murrieta, the Mexican bandit who raised havoc with all the gold miners in the state. It was a great read and attested to Paul's writing talent.

When Paul called to tell me about his book, he mentioned that if it were to be made into a movie, he felt that Eastwood would be the ideal Harry Love. The sad part of this historical novel is that Paul never lived to experience its success. He died a month or two after its publication.

I received a signed copy before his demise. I was touched by the words he expressed regarding our friendship when I saw the personal note that he wrote to me on the first page.

A SALUTE TO THE SPALDING PRO-AM

By Paul Lippman

The Peninsula's Other Great Tournament.

By the time the pros get back to Phoenix (or is it Tucson?), the other great Peninsula golf tournament, the Spalding Pro-Am, already has been played, so not much is said about it during the Crosby, but the real four tuneup of them all deserves a doff of the cap.

The Spalding, a $150,000 event conceived here 11 years ago, has to be the tuneup of them all when we consider that it annually is scheduled the week before the tour starts, regardless the latter dates. This usually brings the event to these Peninsula courses the last week in December, with a finish on January 1st or 2nd.

And what a tuneup it is! The top five finishers at tour-opening Tucson last year all had played the Spalding, among them winner Craig Stadler who has won his first PGA event two out of the three years he's played here.

Stadler, top money player on the 1982 tour, now is a Spalding regular along with defending champion Jay Haas, Bob Gilder, Al Geiberger, John Mahaffey, Johnny Miller, Dave Stockton, Lon Hinkle and, of course, the Peninsula's own Bobby Clampett, who won this event two years ago as an amateur.

Other touring pros who play the Spalding are Kathy Whitworth, Donna Caponi and Patty Sheehan! That's right; the Spalding is for women, too—matter of fact, it's the only tourney in the world where the lady pros compete head-and-head with the men. And how do they do against the guys? Well, Donna Caponi was leading the field by four after 36 a couple of years ago but, alas, had some problems at Pebble Beach in the last round and finished eighth. That's the best any lady pro has done in this unique event. Even so it's good enough for our money just to have Kathy Whitworth show up, for we all know that now she is the greatest of them all in her ranks—top tourney winner in the history of the LPGA with 83 victories. And for added prestige, the phenomenal Juli Inkster, three time U.S. Amateur champion, chose the Spalding this year for her professional debut.

Put these names on the Peninsula's already famous golf courses, and, voilà, we have a world-class event. The tournament is played on three of our finest layouts - Pebble Beach, Carmel Valley Golf and Country Club and Del Monte; with a fourth and final round at Pebble, the ulti-

mate test. The field annually is limited to 270 players, 36 of them touring pros, 54 club professionals and the rest amateurs, whom, top amateurs, it tells us quite enough about the Spalding that 400 other club pros are on the "standby list", and the amateur overflow is staggering, according to tournament director Harold Firstman.

In this year's Spalding, Peter Oosterhuis withstood the charges of defending champion, Jay Haas, Danny Edwards, and Bobby Clampett to snatch the first place prize of $30,000. He played his final round at Pebble in 68, 4 shots under par. Oosterhuis finished at 277. Haas at 278, Edwards at 279, and Clampett at 280, along with Rex Caldwell. The tournament was played in ideal weather conditions and folks were hoping it carries over for the Crosby.

The Spalding was Firstman's 'first-born' (well, almost), a 1977 conception that started as a $25,000 event with no real sponsor except for Hyatt Del Monte Hotel.

"George Roykes, then general manager at the Hyatt, and I put it together as a business stimulant for late December," Firstman recalls, "and it just sort of caught on. Spalding joined us in the fifth year and it's been a big event ever since."

Firstman is considered one of the premier 'golf doctors' on the Peninsula; touring pros call him from all over the country for advice on their problems, and he dispenses the necessary information with the care and meticulous precision of a surgeon. He even runs the Spalding out of a Carmel office that once housed a vascular surgeon—no pun intended.

Harold also is affiliated with Technical Athletic Programs, a San Jose sports management company that quickly is gaining repute in the high-powered world of business athletics.

"We manage all types of athletes," Firstmans says, "but, of course, we're big with the golfers," among them Whitworth, Gilder, Danny Edwards, Keith Fergus, Janet Coles and Sally Little.

Firstman, of course, attends several golf tournaments a year just to consult with and advise his clients, even give them tips on their strokes, "but only if they ask," he is quick to add, for he is that type of golfing gentleman.

Hal was a pro himself for several years, starting at Porter Valley Country Club in Northridge and finishing at Laguna Seca here, though he still advises and consults at Corral de Tierra, where he resides. He also played the tour off and on over the years, but one of the proudest achievements of all was helping Lamar Tech in Beaumont, Texas win three National Intercollegiate championships as a schoolboy golfer.

Lamar Tech? Great golfing college, and few people outside the golf world have heard of the Spalding either, but it's a truly fine tournament—exceptionally well run, as many players are quick to point out - with six prizes that would make a Crosby golfer drool. And that's what it's really all about, isn't it? Good low prizes—and hundred and fifty grand purses.

It's also a 'good gallery' tournament, so the next time you out-of-town visitors are tip-king of coming to the Monterey Peninsula for this very colorful Christmas-New Years week, think of the Spalding as an added filip in the old golfing sock.

A big salute from this Crosby magazine to the Spalding Pro-Am tournament, to Jacque Herrick, director of professional relations for the sponsoring company, and, of course, to Harold Firstman, the local professor of golf.

At times, I convinced Paul Lippman to pen a few words for one of my magazines. He wrote for a San Francisco paper prior to coming to Carmel.

Peter Oosterhuis lines up the winning putt that gave him victory in this year's Spalding Pro-Am.

THIS SOUVENIR MAGAZINE PROVIDED **FREE** TO THE PUBLIC BY GOLF & TENNIS WEST MAGAZINE

the Bing Crosby
NATIONAL • PRO • AM
42nd ANNUAL

PEBBLE BEACH, CALIFORNIA
FEBRUARY 3-6, 1983

Cover art of one of the Crosby's magazines I produced. Mark Savee was the artist working with the Bob Wecker firm.

Dear Sam,

Thanks so much for the terrific review of my book and your kind personal thoughts. Very meaningful.

And I especially liked the fact you said you weren't 'patronizing', which would have been easy to do, considering our long friendship.

Like I've said all along, there aren't many of us left, us long ball hitters!

Again, many thanks, old friend and

Paul "The Lip"

To Sam "The Man"

HARRY LOVE

"My main man" and long time friend for a lot of years, also a good writer and the most honest man I've ever known. Continued good writing, my friend, and Good Reading!

Paul

9-20-03

A note from writer, Paul Lippman. Paul was once a partner with Clint Eastwood in the Hog's Breath Inn, Carmel.

THE STRIKE ZONE

There has always been controversy in baseball regarding the strike zone. In 2002 it was the talk of baseball. Baseball enthusiasts felt there was too much variety in the calls by the umpires. What's the saying: "It could be in the eye of the beholder!"

Willie Mays, who had a good golf game and was very competitive, was visiting Carmel with his close friend Lee Cypress, who had a Don membership at Rancho Cañada, and this is where we met. The Dons were the first members of the club when Nick Lombardo built the two golf courses at the mouth of Carmel Valley.

Lee and Willie were sitting at a table in the dining area. At the time I was writing a column for the *Monterey County Post* called *The Carmel Voice*. I thought it natural to approach Willie and get some comments from one of the greatest baseball hitters of all time. I had access to both of them because I knew them and had played golf with them prior to this meeting.

Willie was not only a great baseball player, but he could hold his own with any amateur golfer. His baseball skills transferred to his golf game…swing, strength, and follow through.

Willie was always friendly to those he knew and cautious with strangers. Many celebrities feel the same way, worried about all the kooks confronting them daily.

I walked over to the table where Lee and Willie sat, had some coffee, and conversed a little. When I got Willie in a talkative mood, I presented him with the question of the day. I said, "Willie, there's been quite a bit of conversation in baseball this year about the strike zone, too many different interpretations by umpires in both leagues. What are your thoughts regarding the strike zone?"

Willie looked at me as only Willie could and replied, "When I played ball, the pitcher threw the ball, and I hit it! End of story."

One of the advantages of living on the Monterey Peninsula is the fact that you can meet many celebrities, some of whom are athletes of the day.

Lee Cypress introduced me to Willie Mays. It was a match between those two and my partner and me. My partner for the match was Ken Farnsworth, the bartender at Rancho Cañada who was well known in the Fresno area for excelling in many sports.

Farnsworth was my partner, and he and I succeeded in ripping their knickers to the tune of one hundred dollars per man. Ken shot 80, I had 8l, Willie scored a 82, and Lee an 89. Well, Willie wasn't a happy camper losing to a bartender and a broadcaster. He scrutinized the score card to make sure it was correct.

We went in for drinks and settled our debts. Farnsworth had to work the next day because this was the last of his two days off.

To my surprise, Willie Mays showed up the next day for a re-match, so to speak. Well, I was hampered because my partner had to work, but Willie insisted on the re-match. The new partner I chose was Bob Harris, a retired school teacher who was a good golfer, but I wasn't comfortable with him. Willie said his partner was a 12 handicap.

We played the West Course at Rancho Cañada, the tougher of the two courses. The result was this: Willie's partner shot an even par 72. Bob Harris and I thought we had been snookered….a 12 handicap shooting even par on a strange course?

We paid off, but weren't happy doing so. Willie made amends for the day before. Hmmm….a l2 handicap? Sure!

To supplement my income and keep my creative juices alive, I started producing magazines for various events held on the Monterey Peninsula. It was part of journalism, I thought, and was part of my media experiences.

There are many events on the Peninsula - golf tournaments, Jazz Festival, the Big Sur Marathon, and many others - and they can only get proper exposure in magazine form. I concentrated more on golf events and published two jazz magazines at the time the Monterey Jazz Festival was held. My partner in the jazz magazine was Johnny Adams, who worked with me at KRML as my program director. His forte was jazz, and he was instrumental in the idea for that publication.

We always hired the best graphics people and the best printers who had experience in producing top quality magazines. The official magazines featuring these said events, often were of inferior quality to our magazines. In fact, we caused them to improve their publications. Never once did they call our company and offer to have us join their staff and to help improve their product. During my years in Las Vegas, there was a constant demand for better talent. On the Monterey Peninsula, however, fresh new talent often frightened the entrenched magazines. I'm pleased to say that we survived despite the defensiveness and negativity.

The selling point with most of our magazines was the cover art. Enjoy some of the cover art from our previous magazines:

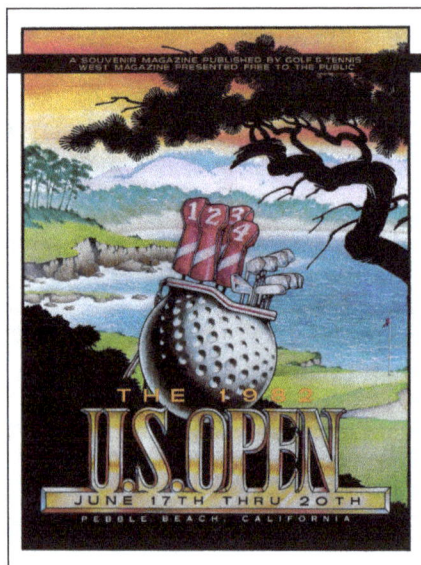

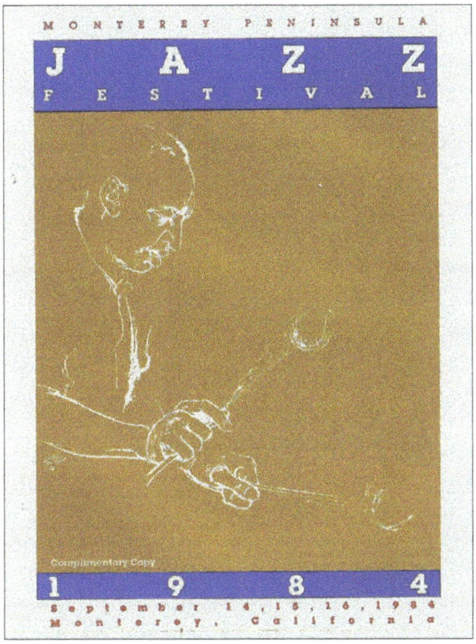
MONTEREY PENINSULA
JAZZ
FESTIVAL
Complimentary Copy
1984
September 14, 15, 16, 1984
Monterey, California

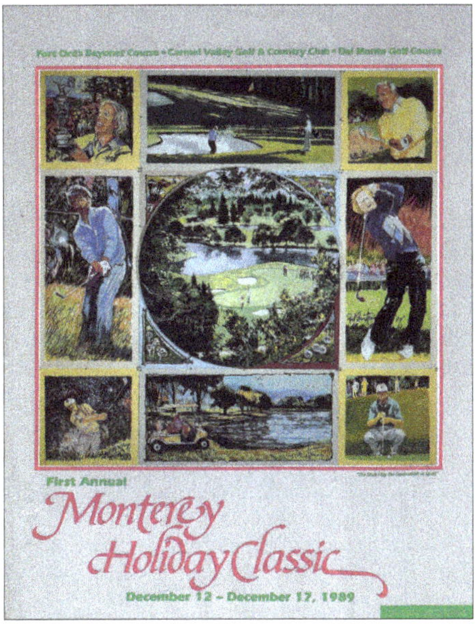
Fort Ord's Bayonet Course • Carmel Valley Golf & Country Club • Del Monte Golf Course
First Annual
Monterey Holiday Classic
December 12 – December 17, 1989

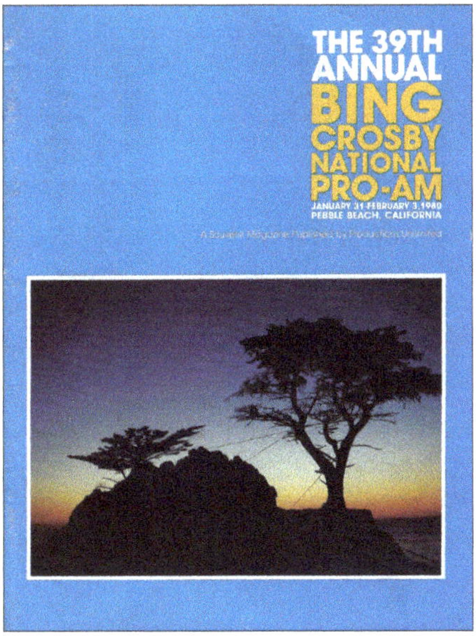
THE 39TH ANNUAL
BING CROSBY NATIONAL PRO-AM
JANUARY 31-FEBRUARY 3, 1980
PEBBLE BEACH, CALIFORNIA

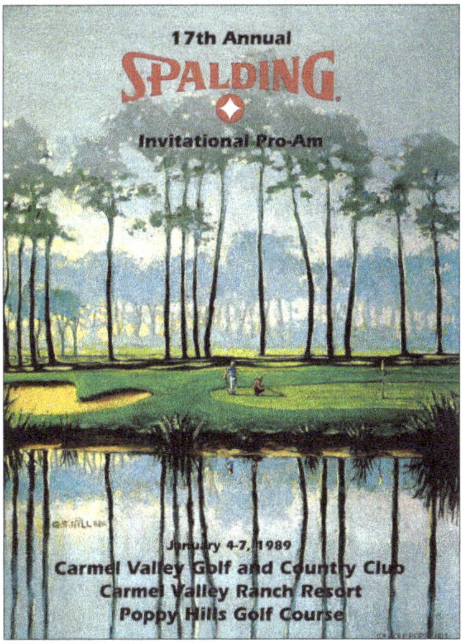
17th Annual
SPALDING
Invitational Pro-Am
January 4-7, 1989
Carmel Valley Golf and Country Club
Carmel Valley Ranch Resort
Poppy Hills Golf Course

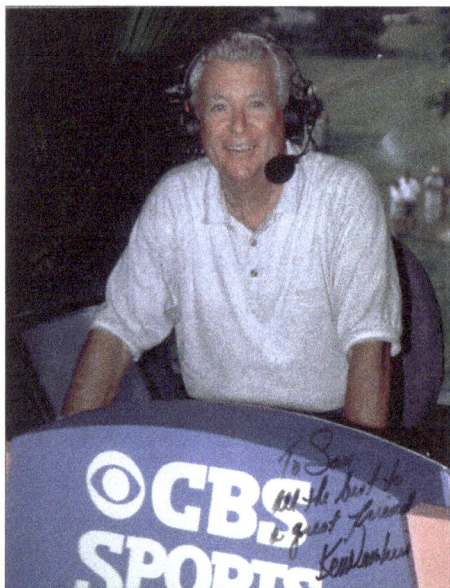

There are many advantages of being a media person, and I have felt privileged all these years because of the people I've met and associated with. One such person whom I met when he was in his prime and one of the top golfers on the PGA tour, playing against the likes of Arnold Palmer, Gary Player, and Jack Nicklaus. All the aforementioned were easy to interview and never turned down a member of the press, before or after a round of golf, whether they played well, or had a miserable round.

Ken Venturi and I became friends when I worked for Louis Prima and both had played together. All but a few of the band members were golfers, Sam Butera and Rollie Dee included in that group.

When I moved to the Monterey Peninsula, Venturi and I spoke many times, when he was playing and winning, or when he was behind the microphone with Jim Nantz for CBS.

On one occasion, Ken was playing Cypress Point, and he showed me some golf shots with a sand wedge, how to move the ball from left to right, and vice versa. Ken was one of the best shot makers in the game, until he suffered wrist problems that stymied his career.

Ken's dad, who was the head pro at Harding Park in San Francisco, was responsible for his golf prowess. Ken was good friends with Ben Hogan, Byron Nelson, and Bing Crosby, and was a regular in the Bing Crosby Pro-Am, later to become the AT&T Pro-Am. Venturi attributes much of his golf shots by Hogan and Nelson and also to his former boss in San Francisco, Ed Lowery. Ed later purchase Beattie Ford in Monterey and joined the Cypress Point Golf Course.

My radio partner, Dave Marzetti, and I conducted many interviews with Venturi; he never once turned us down. A good portion of today's athletes and celebrities can learn from people like the late Ken Venturi, who was always willing to share a microphone for a chat with newspaper reporters so they could fill their columns. Ken Venturi was one of a kind, and he'll be remembered for being always hospitable.

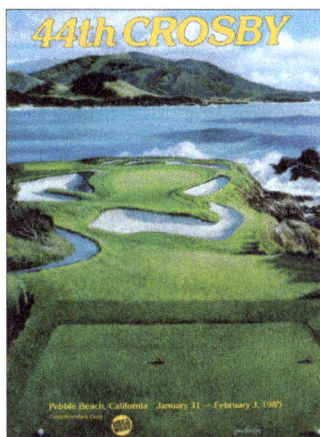

Since I've been a member of the press, I've had many opportunities to play golf at excellent golf courses through my media connections.

The James Peter Cost Gallery was located on Dolores Street, near Sixth Street in Carmel. Mr. Cost specialized in ocean scenes and country scenes with an emphasis on old barns.

Mr. Cost was a member of the Monterey Peninsula Country Club and a pretty good golfer who loved the game. He was friendly enough to invite me as his guest on one occasion and carried with him an application form to entice me to become a member at MPCC. At the time, membership fees were $5,000 to join. Today, it's $250,000 and above. The membership rises regularly.

We played our round and went into the clubhouse to tally the score and to have a cocktail. I don't remember our scores, but I'm certain J-P (as we called him), had outdone me on the course.

I was getting some weird looks from some of the members whom I didn't know, and I felt uncomfortable. At the time, I was a member at Rancho Cañada Golf Club at the mouth of Carmel Valley. At our course, members were down to earth and not snobby. They too were successful business people and didn't feel a need to flaunt their position.

I told Mr. Cost that I wasn't interested in joining the club even though at the time I could afford the fee. The two courses at MPCC (Dunes & Shore) were better recognized than the two courses at Rancho Cañada, but nonetheless, I was happy at Rancho Cañada.

Being the producer of the official *Spalding Invitational Golf Tournament Magazine*, I hired James Peter Cost to paint two covers, one the l5th hole at Cypress Point, and the other the 13th hole at Spyglass Hill. Each painting was a masterpiece and well received.

Mr. Cost retired to Maui, and his legacy is carried on by his daughter, Shelly, a fine painter whose works are shown at Pebble Beach.

One of the best non-touring professional golfers ever was Claude Harmon, host pro at Winged Foot, New York. Claude was a close friend of Ben Hogan and renown as one of the finest teaching pros. His sand game was second to none.

In addition to his teaching prowess, Claude was also a great player. He was the only club pro ever to win the Masters – so far – and he did it in 1948.

Since his death, his sons have illuminated the Harmon name by being teaching gurus for some of the top professional golfers.

Claude gave instruction at Howard Firstman's Golf Clinic in Pebble Beach, and he was very popular. He was very humorous and didn't like how present golf pros taught the rudiments of golf; he was from the old school.

He related this incident to Firstman's son, Jeff, and me. Claude received a telegram from the King of Morocco who needed a lesson. A ticket was sent to Claude and his wife, and they flew to Morocco.

At the driving range the King was ready for his lesson. He got at the address position about to tee off. He was stopped by Claude who remarked to the King: "Now, you remember that ball and that club does not know that you are the King of Morocco."

Harmon logic and humor.

LET ME GO GET THE GIRLS

Clint Eastwood and I have been friends for a long time, even before he made the movie *Play Misty For Me* at KRML some 36 years ago.

We played many rounds of golf at Cypress Point Golf Club with another close friend, Steve King. Steve and I first met in the early '70's, when he was a waiter at The Butcher Shop, a famous restaurant on Ocean Avenue in Carmel. It's now called The Grill on Ocean Avenue. And as I said earlier, our golf games at Cypress included the late Phil Dacey and Jim Freeman.

We all socialized at the Hog's Breath Inn in Carmel, a swingin' place which Clint owned. Everyone who was anyone was on hand nightly. It was the in spot of Carmel. On Christmas day in 1986 when my mother passed away, Clint consoled me that day when we played golf. That night he invited my son Sam Jr. and me to dinner in Carmel Valley.

Another special night, I cooked at Steve King's house, and Clint joined us because he liked our cooking.

While Clint was there he realized that Steve had two cockatiel birds. So did Clint. Apparently he was interested in mating his cockatiels with Steve's. Clint remarked, "Let me go get the girls!" He meant his birds.

Less than a half hour later, Clint returned with his cockatiels in a cage. I commented to Clint that I didn't think any lovemaking would take place, unlike dogs who pick up the scent of dog in heat and commence mating.

As predicted, nothing happened, and Clint left with his cage of cockatiels.

I think we were more disappointed than the girls.

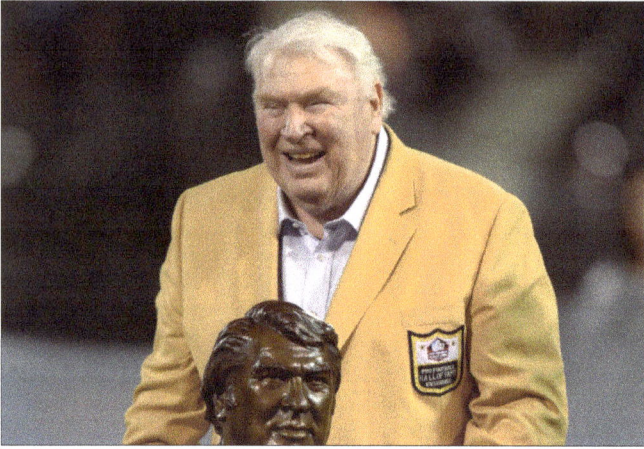

I was introduced to John Madden by Lee Leidig when he was managing the Village Corner Restaurant in Carmel. I was living just across the street from this convenient eating place and spent a good deal of time there.

Madden was still announcing professional football and had purchased a couple of homes in Carmel. He was close friends with Lee and a few other local businessmen. Madden made the Village Corner one of his haunts and brought in his entourage to sit, dine, and chat.

I wasn't part of their regular card games, but I did join them for coffee chats. Those chats generally were, as you might expect, centered around sports. John could relate stories with the best of them, and he was always open for discussions, particularly about the sports happenings of the day, whether football, baseball, golf, or basketball. He had a great knowledge of all sports, even though his expertise was in football.

His wife, Virginia, was interested in preserving the Soldiers Club at Fort Ord, which was located on the ocean side and was beginning to erode badly. She gave me information on it and I ran some mentions in my column "The Carmel Voice." But all her efforts and my few couldn't prevent the demolition of this great club and dance hall. We did try our best.

John has retired from his football chores but can still be heard on radio in the Bay Area. We haven't touched bases for awhile. but on occasion he makes an appearance in Carmel. He was the best as a football analyst and with one of the most recognizable voices in the business.

John Madden, a true American icon.

About 15 years ago, I was approached by Dave Marzetti, a broadcaster who was hosting a show from the Del Monte Golf Course grill, to be a guest on the one-hour radio talk show. I agreed to be on the show, and it was a good experience. Dave and I became acquainted when we covered the AT&T Golf Tournament at Pebble Beach. He was working for KOCN, and I was free-lancing on KNRY, Monterey.

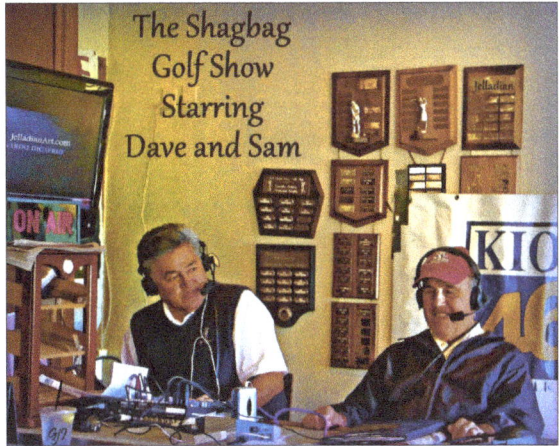

Dave had one booth in the press room and I had an announce booth next to his. We would share interviews. If he had a sound bite that I didn't have, he would loan me the voice actuality. The same was true if he needed one that I possessed.

Well, one show led to another, and after three shows, I became his co-host of the show. It's been running, at this writing, for 15 years. It is heard on KION Radio, l460 on the dial, and we stream live on the Internet *http://shagbagshow.com.* The show is heard each Saturday at 9 a.m. Pacific.

Since we joined forces, Dave and I have been to a good deal of press outings. We covered the AT&T Golf Tournament and have covered each of the U.S. Opens held at Pebble Beach.

The Shagbag Show is the highest rated weekend program on KION, and we're delighted to know our efforts have paid off. Dave is responsible for lining up the interviews and works a month in advance.

Since our association began, we've been very close and have never had a negative word between us. Working with the same person for many years in some cases presents a problem, but we respect each others talent and that's why we get along.

Dave came to the West Coast from Canton, Ohio, and my family moved to Los Angeles during World War 11, from Bristol, Pennsylvania. We both feel that the Monterey Peninsula is the greatest spot in the world. We play golf together and love our Italian wines.

Media man prefers the comforts of home to the glitz of the big city

SAM SALERNO LOOKS around the restaurant like Jack Nicholson in "Something's Gotta Give," as if expecting to see someone who knows him. It is, after all, the Village Corner on Dolores Street, his haunt, his hangout for some 46 years since he came back to Carmel for good. He used to have a table with his name on it, but the letters have worn off. No need; everybody knows his name. And no need to get up, as guests stop by to say hello in a pretty steady stream.

Salerno is a media man, a radio personality from back in the day when DJs were radio royalty. He didn't just play records, he researched them, so he could reveal things like, "Sinatra sang it last night at the Sands," and who was there and what went down, so his listeners felt like they'd been there, too. And then he spun the vinyl.

Elected student body president of Belmont High School in Los Angeles, Salerno thought he had the hubris and the humor to become a stand-up comedian. But he turned his attention to radio after a friend talked him into enrolling in Don Martin's School of Radio & Television Arts in Hollywood.

"I was in LA during the good years," says Salerno, "when people went there on vacation. When we got around by streetcar, and there was no congestion. Both the landscape and the people were beautiful."

Salerno came to Monterey in the 1950s for an audition to DJ for KNBY radio. He ran the show and attended Monterey Peninsula College for a couple of years.

And then he left for Las Vegas.

For 15 years, he was Sam the Morning Man, spinning records and socializing with celebrities. Having interviewed more glitterati and other people of interest than he can recall, he classified himself as the Larry King of Radio.

"I got to Vegas during the Rat Pack days, an era when disc jockeys were popular," Salerno says. "Hotels would call and say, 'Can you get Ella [Fitzgerald] on your show; have you got time to talk to Frank?' I was invited to two shows a night. It was my job to get out into the excitement, to see and be heard. I'd walk into a club and think, 'I'm here, and you're Sinatra, Dietrich, Dean Martin, Sammy Davis Jr., Liberace, Chevalier.' It was when men wore suits, and women were wrapped in furs. I experienced the best of everything."

When he wasn't spinning records, Salerno was promoting them. And then he got into public relations for band leader Van Alexander, jazz pianist Dorothy Donegan, percussionist and pianist Lionel Hampton, and, eventually, the larger-than-life singer, songwriter and trumpeter Louis Prima.

And then he came back to the Monterey

Great Lives

By LISA CRAWFORD WATSON

Peninsula.

"Coming here needs no explanation," Salerno says. "I've traveled all over the world, and people always ask, 'If you live in Carmel, what are you doing here?' Once you've been here, you know there is no place in the world like it."

Salerno got a house in the Carmel

See LIVES page 27A

LIVES
From page 25A

Highlands neighboring Joan Fontaine, and then he bought KRML radio. It was 1968, and the format was "middle of the road jazz and blues." He stabilized the station by making it an ABC affiliate, and moved into progressive rock. In 1972 KRML rocketed to fame when Salerno's pal Clint Eastwood focused his directorial debut, "Play Misty For Me" on the station. After nine years on the air, Salerno decided his song had played out. He sold the station.

In 1986, says Salerno, Bud Allen approached him to suggest he run for mayor of Carmel. Salerno, who felt his success as student body president did not sufficiently qualify him for the job, said he had to think about it.

"Bud came back and said, 'Never mind — I've found somebody else. Clint's going to run,'" Salerno recalled. "Well I didn't want to run against my buddy, so I worked on Clint's campaign, instead."

These days, Salerno lives in a well-lit studio above the Little Swiss Café, which is just across Sixth Avenue from the Village Corner. After writing a column, The Carmel Voice, for three years, Salerno turned his attention back to radio. In 2002, he and renowned radio personality David Marzetti teamed up to present "The Shagbag Show," a Saturday commentary which airs from their chairs in The Grille restaurant at Old Del Monte Golf Course.

Very little seems to be off topic during the hour-long talk show, which may include retail and restaurants, music and movies, food and wine, cars and cigars, travel and tourism and, by all means, golf.

Sitting in his nook at the Village Corner, beneath a cap that reads 2011 U.S. Open, Salerno continues to wave or nod to passersby, both inside and outside the restaurant. Some linger at the table to joke with him or make plans for later. He greets everyone by name.

"I know everybody in town, and we've shared a lot of good times over the years. The key to my longevity," he says, referring to his relationships and his life, "is to act young, make sure to stand up, watch your diet, and play a lot of golf.

To suggest someone for this column, email emgiuliano@gmail.com.

Salerno in the broadcast studio at KRML in 1972, when he was the station's colorful owner.

One gentleman I've enjoyed a great deal is Jim Tunney, who is known in sporting circles as the Dean of NFL referees. Jim has come on *The Shagbag Show* many times to promote various local events that raise money for charity. While he is on the show, Jim makes for good copy because he relates many interesting anecdotes from his NFL years concerning various athletes and certain interesting plays that took place during those years.

Having been raised in Southern California as I was, we have a good deal in common regarding that part of the country. I went to Belmont High, and I think he went to Eagle Rock, in the same league.

101
Best of Tunney
Side of Sports Columns

Dr. Jim Tunney
"Dean of NFL Referees"

COACHES ≡CHOICE

www.jimtunney.com
m@jimtunney.com

When he retired, Jim made Pebble Beach his home. He has meshed beautifully with the Monterey Peninsula, giving motivational speeches, and supporting many local charities. With his input on any given charity, you know it's going to be successful.

To further his expertise in the world of sports, Jim has written a regular weekly column in the *Monterey County Herald* entitled, "The Tunney Side of the Street!"

Jim Tunney has many friends in the sporting world and corporate world, and it's always an audience builder when he appears on our radio show. He has appeared regularly on *The Shagbag Show* when we broadcast live from the pro shop during the AT&T Golf Tournament. He's the quality kind of guy who makes it worthwhile being in the profession. It's always a blessing to know great people, and Jim happens to be a great American and communicator.

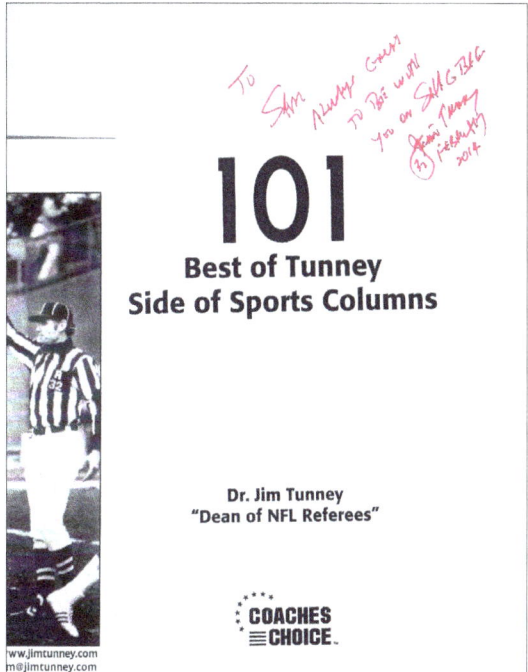

SOME ADDITIONAL WRITINGS

MY WRITING YEARS

I have always had a desire to write, since I was in the ninth grade and Mrs. Kennedy was introducing us to Shakespeare and other great writers. She tried to teach us what was good about reading the right books and retaining the knowledge for the future, whatever your endeavor.

Later it was Mrs. Hov at Belmont High School in Los Angeles who was also an instigator in teaching me to write, whether it was sports or other types of communicating through the written word. At Belmont, I wrote for the school newspaper, *The Belmont Sentinel*. Also in our class was Murray Fromson, who went to CBS Radio and was a foreign correspondent for years. When he retired he began teaching at University of Southern California in Los Angeles.

At Monterey Peninsula College, under the tutelage of Mel Huden I wrote feature articles during my tenure there. *El Yanqui* was the newspaper.

In Las Vegas, I wrote for *Panorama Newspaper* and was the Las Vegas stringer for *Deejay Magazine*, a national monthly magazine. At the radio stations I worked for or those I also managed, I wrote commercial copy, news stories, or commentaries. It was no chore, because I was schooled properly and learned on the job. As with all professions, repetition helped to perfect my writing skills.

It was inevitable that I would write my memoirs after all these years behind a typewriter and now on a computer.

April 6, 1945

Marshall, Franklin Turn In Fair Pre-Season Times . . .

BY SAM SALERNO

Out Marshall way they have just recently completed their inter-class track meet. For pre-season, the boys did "all reet," but we must not forget our fellows at Crown Hill and their times.

In the 660-yard run the best time was 1:32.5 made by Chick Drylie. Kirkman did 1:34.5; Rhodes, 1:36.5; and Alonzo Gibbs, 1:38.

So, you can readily see the 660 will be no pushover for Messrs. Winston, Wolfson, and Gonzales of Belmont.

In the 1320, Don Rodella breezed through a 3:42.5, which is fairly good. Our own Gene Arellano has done 3:39 twice this season.

Marshall's Eads cannot compare with Belmont's Lyons in the B high jump. He has done 5 feet 2 inches while Lyons has reached easily place in the City Meet this

5 feet 7 inches.

The last B event on which your scribe has definite information is the shot put in which Gallasso heaved the put 39 feet 4 inches, which is an average first in any meet.

Marshall Speedsters

Nick Giovinazzo nosed out Pat Fazio in the century dash in 10.5.

Dick Gold recently ran the 70-yard high hurdles in 9.5, as a result of a flying start.

Bob Arbon, who placed first in last year's City Meet 660, ran the half mile in 2:14.5, and his time is decreasing weekly.

Outstanding performer for the Marshall tracksters is returning monogram wearer, Mart Scisorek. Recently, he tossed the 12-pound shot 46 feet 11½ inches. He should easily place in the City Meet this

season.

That's enough for Marshall at the moment; we'll see and hear plenty about them when the time comes.

Panthers Show Promise

Over at Franklin, a host of Panthers burn up the cinderpaths.

In an invitational practice meet recently, Dick Moje ran a 4:44.3 mile, taking a third place against fellows from S. C. and Glendale.

Promising newcomers for the Panthers are Loren Bennett in the broad jump, Ed Harmon in the 220, Lin Younger, (ex-660) and Buddie Beadle doing their turn at the 440 yard dash. However, altogether the prospects do not look bright.

Belmont can expect keen competition in the Northern League this season.

Letter Writing Now 1 A on Crown Hill

BY SAM SALERNO

"Say, do you have an airmail stamp, Betty?"

"There's one around here someplace, but what's the big rush, Susie?"

"Oh, I gotta get this letter off to Bob. He's in France, you know".

"Hey, help me with this spelling, will yuh? I'm writing to Johnny and he's such a brain I hafta have this spelled right."

And so on and on chat the girls of Belmont, for times have changed. (Ask any commercial teacher).

Time was when letter writing was an unknown or at least unpracticed art hereabouts, but not since the war. Now it has risen to first-rate importance with the gals. (Query: Do boys ever write to G. I.'s?)

Today it's not books that the girls carry to classes, nor homework they do after school—no, writing to the boys in khaki and blue takes up most of their time, especially in school, and especially in class. These girls are equipped with pen, ink, envelopes (perfumed), and blotters, plus lipstick for kisses on their letters.

What we want to know, is when do the gals find time to study in addition to writing twenty letters a week? How about letting the fellows in on the system? Or maybe we can guess: you don't study.

Boles Drive Inn
8-13-50
One reading on Sat. & Sun.--baseball game
Sam Salerno

A new feature has been added at Boles Drive
Inn announces its new owner, Elmer Peacock.
Delicious chicken, hamburger, and shrimp
in the basket. Mr. Peacock says, "that
our shrimp is guaranteed not to snap back".
Gourmets of fine food all agree that
dinning at Boles Drive Inn is indeed a
pleasure. Dine where eating "Boles" over
the most squimish appetite---at Boles Drive
Inn between the juction of highway 111 and
99. Car service is available from 6 on.
Remember, Indio's first is still the finist!!

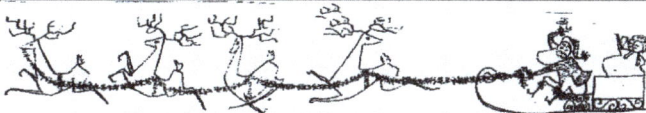

Merry Christmas and a Happy New Year

EL YANQUI

Vol. 5 No. 7   Monterey Peninsula College, Monterey, California   Friday, Dec. 19, 1952

ity Acts To Reduce Accident Danger At MPC

New Freeway, Stoplight Lessen Traffic Hazard

by Sam Salemo and Johnny Adams

The State of California has granted the City of Monterey nearly a half million dollars to construct a four-lane divided highway, with limited access adjoining thoroughfares, to better regulate the flow. of traffic on Fremont Extension and, in part, at least, to insure the safety of students at the Monterey Peninsula College.

Cost of Safety Comes High

With the new proposed freeway the chances of safety will be greatly increased, says Walter Hahn, City Manager of Monterey. It has been proved that 35 miles per hour is the speed at which motorists can sensibly think and act. Three signal lights are to be installed, one at the entrance of the Monterey Peninsula College, controlling incoming and outgoing traffic, another at the General Line school, an intersection which at the present time is very dangerous, and the third at the Salinas cutoff. Mr. Hahn further states that with such safety features as these, and a divided highway, we will avoid what he called, "VERY DESTRUCTIVE ACCIDENTS," as those shown in the picture at the bottom of the page.

The state's proposal for the freeway calls for a four lane divided highway with limited access highways on each side. Anything less, according to state officials, would not handle the traffic load. The cost of $400,000 will be solely financed by the state. Consequently, the freeway will be built according to state specifications.

Police Chief Charles Simpson says the rate of accidents per million miles should be cut to one quarter.

This decision of the state followed action by the city council on December 2 approving the project by a 3-2 vote after the city planning commission, after protracted study, was unable to make a recommendation, voting 4-4 on the proposition that certain streets in Oak Grove be cut off from direct access to the new freeway.

City Manager Walter Hahn and Chief of Police Charles Simpson, in discussing this improvement with your two El Yanqui reporters, stated that 20,000 automobiles daily travel past the college entrance and, with the expected influx of population to the Peninsula, this number will increase to more than 40,000 in four years.

Chief Simpson made it clear that the new freeway would easily handle this number even at the proposed speed limit of 35 miles per hour and with traffic slowed down by stop lights at strategic intersections. A stop light at the college entrance will facilitate the movement of traffic from the college at busy hours. It is expected that the construction of the freeway will take from six months to a year, according to Mr. Hahn.

Inside Las Vegas

By SAM SALERNO
KLAS — Las Vegas

Back again like the man who tried to get even on the tables in our city! A great deal is happening, hope we're not redundant . . . first, another strip hotel opens. It's the **Sans Souci** whose publicist is **Don Holiday**, formerly of KORK. Good luck, Don, on the promotion. Speaking of KORK, we're happy to report that **Dick Goldring** has found his niche in life. Dick's one of their newer disk jockeys and is new to the radio game but not to show biz, having sung with various vocal groups. In his spare hours, he's helping papa at their Pub (I say) on Main Street.

Vegas Radio Hop-Skip and Jumps

Don Adams at KLAS from KBMI . . . **Gus Giuffre** moved from KRBO to KRAM with an afternoon show, also works nites at KSHO-TV. Who needs sleep? **Gil Bogos** at KSHO as is **Jim Taraldson** who spent the summer with the AEC. **Jean Paul King** is managing this TV outlet for **Merv Addleson.** When you read this, they will have moved to their El Rancho Hotel location. **Roland Vaile** and **Bob Janes** purchase KTOO radio in Henderson, Nevada. Roland gave up post with Chamber of Commerce in making the move. Jane was formerly in San Francisco prior to his Las Vegas stint. . .

Bill Daly of this mag phoned me from Indianapolis to tell me he'd be in Vegas for his wife's birthday. Incidentally, Bill's wife happens to be **Annie Maloney** and she's currently featured in the lounge at the Silver Slipper. **Russ Hickman** of KLAS nursing a slashed chin. No, it wasn't Gentleman **Gene Delmont** of the Thunderbird who clipped him. He tangled with his dog and a sharp piece of glass. Result? Five stitches!

**Proud Papa Department —
(And Mama)**

Louise and **Martin Black** cheering the arrival of baby boy. Martin hosts the late movie on KLRJ-TV . . . **Ted McKinstry** of KRAM also passing out cigars upon arrival of his 2nd boy; now has 2 boys and 2 girls. **Jay Davis** of KRBO becomes pappa-san for time number two. I'd better steer clear of these boys — it could be catching! . . . **Harvey Diederich** in at Hotel Sahara in the publicity department. He'll work with **Herb MacDonald** and **Larry Sloan** . . . The 1957 edition of the **Sahara Cup Races** at Lake Mead drew between 30 and 40,000. This year's event was won by **Jack Regas** in the Hawaii Kai. Jack also won top honors last year . . . KINK-TV in Seattle covered the event filming segments of the proceeding. This info was forwarded to your reporter by **Johnny Gunn** of KENO who used to work for KING. **John Romero** wrote about it for Sports Illustrated.

Talk about a relaxing disk jockey, **Joe Graydon** of KENO broadcasting on a Riviera convertible sofa bed. He was escorted down the strip by cohorts **Harry Anderson, Bob Bailey,** and **Don Broughman.** I guess you have to have a gimmick, eh? . . . **Jerry Dexter** hosting an early a. m. show from the El Cortez Hotel. **Jack Kogan** initiated the show but his publicity chores keep him pre-occupied. . . . **Hank Penny** and his Mrs. (**Sue Thompson**) in to our studios to inform us of their new Golden Nugget Show. Hank's a riot as evidenced by his appearance on **Art Mooney's Talent Train** show from the Royal Nevada Hotel. KLAS-TV telecasts it on Channel 8 . . . **Hank Smith** has taken over **Jean Paul King's** ad agency and doing a commendable job.

KRAM dee jay's broadcasting from the Mobile Home Show at Cashman Field. One trailer was converted into a unique little studio. **Hal Morelli** had trouble stretching his "daddy long legs". This boy's a gas when he commences to make with the ad-libs. . . **King Harmon** still taking requests on his KORK western show aired in the morning hours an hour before we hit the ther waves . . . Listened to **Vince Brascia** and **Rick Richardson** on a football broadcast from Yerrington. These two have been long-time favorites in Henderson expressing a keen desire of what happens in Nevada's third largest city. . , **Joe Julian** of KRBO paying **Len Ross** a visit in Santa Barbara. . . Well, that'll have to do for this month . . . gotta run along. Look me up if you all get to Vegas. . . Bye for now.

Paul Masson
Summer Series '83
in it's 26th year
salutes
the

Monterey Jazz
Festival '83

For information please write to:
Paul Masson Summer Series '83
P.O. Box 1852
Saratoga CA 90570

Stephane Grappelli and Oscar Peterson

By Sam Salerno

July 4th is reserved for fireworks and for the patrons of the arts, the bombasting of sounds emanating from the hills of Saratoga, California, was far more exciting than a fireworks display. Those sun worshippers and music lovers were treated to American music by two foreign entertainers. It was JAZZ with a capital J in its purist form, performed by two of the world's greatest artists, Stephane Grappelli from France and Oscar Peterson from Canada.

The scene was the Paul Masson Mountain Winery in the hills of Saratoga, where a packed house (outdoors) braved the heat of summer to revel in the "sounds" of Grappelli and Peterson! It was labeled the "Vintage Sounds" 1983, one of many concerts offered by the Paul Masson Mountain Winery.

The Oscar Peterson Trio was first on stage and kept everyone spellbound with their interpretations of "Lush Life," Duke Ellington's "Satin Doll," "Solitude," and "Caravan." Unmistakably, the influence of Art Tatum could be heard in the nimble fingers of Peterson, who made his United States debut in 1949 in "Jazz at the Philharmonic," and whom some music critics say "plays too many notes." I agree, he does play too many notes, but who can play them as well?

His style is that of Tatum, running up and down the keyboard, blending chords, and spending a good deal of time in the bass range. Peterson consumes the piano and it's like putty in his hands. He can stretch a note, or can roll it up in a ball and toss it! Without a doubt, he is the most prolific jazz artist in the world. One wonders why he doesn't warble a tune as he did years ago, emulating the vocal stylings of the late Nat King Cole?

The first hour was gone after "The One O'clock Jump," "Body and Soul," and an original called "On Danish Shore." The trio took its bows and the master of ceremonies gave a speech commemorating the 75th birthday of Stephane Grappelli. The winery offered champagne and carrot cake for everyone during the intermission.

Both Oscar Peterson and Stephane Grappelli received the "key" to the city of San Jose.

After the refreshment break, Stephane Grappelli appeared on stage with his group, consisting of two guitars and a bass. They kicked off their set with "Cheek to Cheek," "Them There Eyes," an up tempo version of "Shine," the Frankie Laine hit of some years back, "After You've Gone," and "Sweet Georgia Brown." Martin Taylor was guitar soloist on "Shine" and "Old Man River."

This was the final week of a four month tour for Grappelli who is heading back to Paris. Grappelli was founder of the group known as The Quintet of the Hot Club of France. He and guitarist, Django Reinhardt, were responsible for forming the group in the early 30s. It became one of the swingingest combos from Europe to make its sounds felt around the world through the advent of recordings and radio broadcasts.

Grappelli and Peterson have worked together on recordings but during this appearance did not play together, much to the surprise of everyone.

After a standing ovation, Grappelli returned to delight the enthusiastic crowd with a Gershwin medley and upon conclusion, in his perfect French, he uttered, "merci, merci!"

Thank you, Paul Masson Winery, for allowing us to sample your fine wine and for bringing such great talent to California. Merci!

A musical review I wrote in 1983 concerning the appearance of Stephane Grappelli at the Paul Masson Winery.

A musical review I wrote in 1983 concerning the appearance of
Stephane Grappelli at the Paul Masson Winery.

By SAM SALERNO
KLAS - Las Vegas, Nevada

Congratulations are in accord for **Bea Terry** and her new staff of Deejay Magazine.

Now every dee jay in the country within reading distance should inform his fellow platter spinner to peruse this popular magazine, the only one of its kind. THANKS!!!

Now about Las Vegas and what's been happening. At this writing, the NBA (National Boxing Association) members are meeting in our city to map out strategy for the coming year. Rumored that **Cus D'Amato, Patterson's** manager, will kiss and make up with IBC.

Vegas radio reaped the benefits of the primary elections and will pick up some more green gold in November during the finals. Three radio members ran for office: **Joe Julian** of KRBO for County Assessor, **Jack Lehman**, free-lancer announcer for Assembly, and **Halley Gates** of KRAM news department ran for **Marryin' Sam** (Justice of the Peace). We regret to report that each candidate was defeated.

KRAM sold to a group which also owns KIST in Santa Barbara. **Larry Buskett**, Prexy, says no changes are in the offing. . . **Fred Von Hofen** in Oregon managing a station after Sherwood of KENO, Las Vegas . . . **Don Adams**, formerly of KLRJ-TV spinning crazy disks at KENO . . . **BOB BOCK**, who came to Nevada to be a silver miner and found he didn't have the "pan" for it, now dee jaying on KLAS Radio. Bob's from Long Island, N.Y. Ironically, he shows no traces of locale in his speech . . . bravo!

VACATIONING . . .

Rob Thomas of WEMP in Milwaukee in to visit us . . . He flew his own plane out West; an interesting chap. . . **Bob Custer** of KLOK in San Jose, with whom I worked in '52 at that station, back for his second year in a row to take in the local sights. He particularly liked the rave of the strip, "La Lido De Paree" at the Stardust and **Betty Hutton** at the Sahara.

Bill Randle of WERE in Cleveland in town and this dee jay helping him line up a studio for recording a strip hotel group . . . **Jean Paul King**, commuting back and forth from the city of angels to handle his Monitor chores or Vegas. . . **King Harmon** at KORK spending a well-earned vacation . . . **Fred Young**, KRAM, finally getting away for a few days after trying for six years!!!

Down to look over the Vegas radio picture with an eye to buy, **John Miller** of Salt Lake City. John was my boss in '50 and '51 while we worked at KMBY in Monterey. He later sold this station to **Der Bingle**. . . Our thanks to **Kai Webb**, formerly of KOFA in Yuma, Arizona, for the kind words to the editor of this mag.

We have to hurry along but we'll keep you posted like a sign board the next time these eyes meet . . . Bye.

Fabulous Husband -Wife Team

Louis Prima and Keely Smith, the wildest Capitol recording stars, recently did the almost unbelievable.

After completing their midnight to dawn entertaining schedule in the Casbar Theatre of the Hotel Sahara in Las Vegas, where they remain through Oct. 20th, they recorded a new album of twelve tunes; also, two single sides.

Capitol flew Voyle Gilmore and a unit to the desert resort from Hollywood for the session. Then after working another ten hours, with less than two hours of sleep, they reported for make-up and performed before the cameras for Columbia Pictures, doing their "Old Black Magic" sequence in the Harry Romm production of "Senior Prom." A full motion picture filming group trekked to the spa to handle the situation.

The fabulous husband-wife team are rated among Capitol's hottest properties. Out of Hollywood and most of America's top ten selling albums, five are those of Louis Prima and Keely Smith. They are "Las Vegas Prima Style," "The Wildest Show at Tahoe," "The Wildest," "Call of the Wildest" and "I wish You Love."

Keely's album "I Wish You Love" is neck and neck with Frank Sinatra's "Come Fly With Mee' and deejays do raves over it. Later this year, she will do an album with Sinatra.

Early this year, the National Academy of Musical Arts presented Keely with a gold trophy award as "Television's Newest Musical Personality."

Deejay has a new home. Send all mail to new address!

GOLF REFINED TO A TEE

Putting on the Peninsula

By SAM SALERNO
PHOTOGRAPHY By LOUISE BERNSTEN

When the question of golf courses arises in any circle, American or worldwide, Pebble Beach and the Monterey Peninsula enliven the conversation because golf is *not* golf unless it's played here! Sure, the Scots invented the game, but the American golf course designers have refined it to a tee. Nowhere is it more evident than here where the weather, terrain and scenery make it more conducive for a true test of golfing gamesmanship. Its rare beauty awes high handicappers and low-handicap players praise the fairness and difficulty of each golf course. At times, a golfer's attention fades off the ball and draws toward this Pacific peninsula's picturesque views and vistas.

If a survey was taken, **Pebble Beach Golf Links** would rate number one as the most popular of all courses on the Monterey Peninsula. Pebble Beach first opened for play in 1919. The late S.F.B. Morse, owner of Del Monte Properties, predecessor of the Pebble Beach Company, and golf champion Jack Neville first walked about the rugged cliffs overlooking the Pacific and staked out the course. Then, when Pebble Beach was chosen as the site for the 1929 U.S. Amateur Tournament, Chandler Egan was commissioned from Philadelphia to rebuild the greens according to championship specifications.

Pebble remains the site of the AT&T Pro-Am, formerly the Bing Crosby National Pro-Am, and the California State Amateur tournament. It also served as the site of the 1972 and 1982 U.S. Open, the first of which was won by Jack Nicklaus and the last one by Tom Watson — with his memorable chip-in on the 17th hole. It was also the site of the 1977 PGA Championship. Ken Venturi, Gene Littler, Tony Lema, Johnny Miller, Tom Watson, Jack Nicklaus and Bobby Clampett have all cut their teeth at Pebble Beach.

One of the most photographed holes in golf is Pebble's seventh. Normally, it's a half-wedge, wedge, or 9-iron shot (weather permitting) but when the wind blows, pull out a 3-iron or 3-wood; it's *that* unpredictable a hole. Pebble Beach is also a favorite of foreign tourists who have seen it on worldwide television. Golfers from Japan, Scotland and Australia make it a "must" on their golfing vacations. You can tee up starting at 7 a.m. with foursomes playing at 10-minute intervals. Cost is $125 per person, but Lodge guests and forest residents pay $95, carts are included. Caddies are available; pro Steve McLennan — 624-3811.

For the impatient, occasional golfer or the player who wants to perfect his short irons, Pebble Beach Company provides a nine-hole,

par-3 course, **The Peter Hay**. Green fees are $9 for all day. The Pebble Beach Golf Shop can fill your souvenir needs with sweaters, caps, umbrellas, shoes and other golf paraphernalia, all carrying the familiar Pebble Beach logo. The shop is open dawn till dusk (624-3811).

Spyglass Hill, also operated by Pebble Beach Company, offers more favorite fairways. If you're a beginner, Spyglass is not a hacker's course, measuring 6,810 yards from the tips. The course rewards a good shot and penalizes a poor one — the way a course should be designed! There are no 'gimmies' on Spyglass and no gimmicks for fudging scores: you must execute good golf shots! Hole for hole, putt for putt, many consider it the best golf test around. Course management remains the key to a lower score. The first hole from the regular tee logs 551 yards, with a dogleg left. The first five holes gird the baby blue Pacific Ocean. Greens fees are

$60, with carts costing $24. Pro is Bob Hickam. Tee off times start from dawn to dusk. The course is located at Stevenson Drive and Spyglass Hill Road in Pebble Beach.

Reservations for Pebble Beach Company golf courses can be made through Golf Central at 624-3811. To play area courses and arrange motel and hotel reservations contact *Mike Roseto's Wide World of Golf and Travel* (624-6667). Roseto's Carmel company offers more than 27 years of experience in golf travel around the world, including Ireland, Scotland, Europe, Hawaii and Palm Springs, and other golf capitals of the United States.

The newest golf course on the Monterey Peninsula is **Poppy Hills** at Pebble Beach, designed by Robert Trent Jones Jr. and owned by the Northern California Golf Association. Situated in the country club area, the course measures 6,219 yards from the white tees and 6,850 yards from the blues. From the tips, it takes a course rating of 75.9. It's a different golf challenge, with shots based on accuracy and not length. The greens are expansive and undulating and if you're not careful on some greens, you might be looking at four putts. Nor Cal members get a break here with greens fees at $30

and $45 for guests. Carts are only mandatory for non-members, whose greens fees are $60. For reservations call (408) 625-2035 or the pro shop 625-2154.

The Spanish Bay Golf Links, which shares the Pebble Beach Company umbrella, will open November 1987. This links-style course, designed by Tom Watson (his first commissioned course design), Robert Trent Jones Jr. and Sandy Tatum, is designed for 6,872 yards adjacent to The Inn at Spanish Bay.

Cypress Point is perhaps the most meticulously manicured course situated on the popular 17-Mile Drive, near Pebble. If God offered a die-hard golfer one last round before the 19th hole, he'd choose Cypress Point. The most famous hole at Cypress is the treacherous 16th, 233 yards over an ocean chasm. Bing Crosby and professional Jerry Pate have made holes-in-one here. Course lessons are provided by host professional Jim Langley, however, Cypress is strictly private.

The exclusive **Monterey Peninsula Country Club** offers two courses — The Dunes and Snore, but must be played with a member. Before Spyglass Hill was designed, it served as a course during the Bing Crosby National Pro-Am. Pro is Art Williams.

The oldest course west of the Mississippi is Pebble Beach's **Del Monte Golf Course**, adjacent to the Hyatt Regency at 1300 Sylvan Road in Monterey. Opened in 1897 and designed by golf and polo enthusiast Charles Maud, the greens challenge champions and are the favorite of local players. Among Del Monte's toughest holes is number 16, the second handicap hole with 417 yards. Better hit a good drive here, or you'll be grabbin' a wood for your second shot. Greens fees — $20 (cart optional). For more information call 373-2436.

A mile from Highway 1 in Carmel Valley is **Rancho Canada Golf Club**, offering 36 public holes with some overlooking Carmel River. The west course measures 6,613 yards with a par 72, and the east is 6,434 yards, par 71. Two tough holes on the east course are the 13th, a 230 yard par 3 that requires a shot over the Carmel River and the 18th, which is 425 yards uphill. If you play in the afternoon, you're hitting your second shot into a stiff wind. Greens fees are $25 weekdays, $28 weekends and holidays, $15 after twilight, with power carts costing $20 (optional). Pro is Paul La Goy, Carmel Valley Road, one mile east of Highway 1 (624-0111).

A mile away from Rancho is **Carmel Valley Golf and Country Club** and Quail Lodge, a five-star resort and restaurant. The golf course, site of the annual Spalding Pro-Am, designed by

Robert Graves, features lakes, sand traps, beautiful fairways and superb greens. The course is always in magnificent condition. It is 6,175 yards in length, par 71. Pro is Laird Small. Open to members of Quail Lodge by reservations. Greens fees $50; Quail Lodge guests, $35. Hours: 7 a.m. to 6:30 p.m. Three miles east of Highway 1, on Carmel Valley Road (624-2770).

Farther into Carmel Valley, about seven miles from Highway 1, is **Carmel Valley Ranch**, opened in 1981 and designed by Pete Dye. The Ranch, as it is known, is private, with both nines offering a variety of golf and a new hotel with spacious rooms and suites under construction on the back nine, adjacent to the 12th hole. The hotel will command an awesome view of the Carmel Valley. The front nine of this course runs along Carmel River and the back nine climbs to heights of 600 to 700 hundred feet. Carts are mandatory and the view, particularly on the back nine, is breathtaking. Pro is Harry Turner, formerly with Landmark at La Quinta in Palm Springs. The Ranch also serves the Spalding Pro-Am. In order to play, you must be a guest of a member. There is also a reciprocal arrangement for members of other Landmark properties. Hours: 8 a.m. to dark. Greens fees are $60,

including cart. One Old Ranch Road, Carmel Valley (625-1010).

Seven miles from Monterey on the Salinas Highway is **Laguna Seca Ranch Golf Club**, another course run by professional Nick Lombardo, who also heads Rancho Canada and Pajaro in Watsonville (Lombardo is also associated with Fig Gardens in Fresno). Laguna Seca is an 18-hole layout designed by Robert Trent Jones Jr., and is open to the general public. Greens fees are $17 weekdays, $23 weekends and holidays, and $10 after twilight. Pacific Golf Group Senior Citizens get a preferred rate on Tuesdays. Carts are $20. On York Road off Monterey Salinas Highway 68 (373-3701).

Closer to Salinas and a few miles from Laguna Seca, **Corral de Tierra Country Club**, a par-72 course, offers a private, secluded haven of rolling hills and oak trees. Corral de Tierra Country Club measures 6,428 yards and many of its members are from the Salinas area. Corral de Tierra also has a reciprocal agreement with other private courses on Thursdays and Fridays. Green fees $40, golf carts $10. Pro Gerry Greenfield. Hours: 7:30 a.m. to 6 p.m. Ten miles east of Monterey (372-6244).

If you're looking for a sporty, links-type course, where shot making is more important than length, then **Pacific Grove Golf Links** is your best bet. It's an 18-hole public course with one of the most spectacular views around . . . and the price is right. The front nine borders on the ocean and the back nine is inland. Pacific Grove was carved out of a sand dune by Jack Neville, who also designed Pebble Beach Golf Links. Greens fees are $10 weekdays, $12 weekends, carts $16 — optional. Pro is Pete Vitarisi. Asilomar Boulevard, Pacific Grove (375-3456).

Situated on six beautiful acres with cascading waterfalls and impeccable landscaping, **Seacliff Inn** is located only three blocks from Seacliff State Park. Offering a special golf package at four courses, De Laveaga, Pajaro, Pasatiempo and Seascape, Seacliff Inn provides luxury golf at economy prices. Desired starting times are requested two weeks in advance and must be verified with the individual golf course. For more information for combined golf and room rates, call 688-7300.

The Navy Golf Course, adjacent to the Monterey County Fairgrounds, allows civilians to play as guests of the military. It's 18 holes with a par 69. Green fees are $6 weekdays, $7 weekends; guests $8 weekdays, $10 weekends. Greens fees good all day with carts $10. Weekdays, 7:30 a.m. till 7 p.m. Weekends, 6:30 a.m. to 7 p.m. Manager Bob Moffatt (646-2167).

Fort Ord, with two courses — Bayonet and Black Horse, can also be played with military personnel. Carts are optional on all military courses.

In our surrounding communities, you will find other golf courses in Salinas, Watsonville, Aptos and Santa Cruz, all within a 30-mile range. There is a course designed for every game and every budget. See you on the first tee! □

"In Carmel a shop you must visit." — *Golf Digest*

Golf Arts & Imports

All about golf. Finest selection of prints or originals, books, clubs, silver, porcelains, and crystal — both antique and new. Sweaters and caps from Scotland. Vast collection of distinctive golf gifts. Ask for our catalogue.

CATALOGUE
GOLF ARTS & IMPORTS
CARMEL, CALIFORNIA

GOLF

GOLF ARTS & IMPORTS

Operated by Michael C. Roseto
of Wide World of Golf

Dolores St. at 6th
P.O. Box 5217
Carmel, Ca. 93921
(408) 625-4488
Open daily at 10 a.m.

CARMEL VOICE *by Sam Salerno*

Sam Salerno by Bill Bates

Today I want to toot my horn on behalf of **Pete Rose** at a time when new members are inducted into the Baseball Hall of Fame. Those honored were Orlando Cepeda, Robin Yount, George Brett, and Nolan Ryan. Pete Rose, **former Cincinnati great**, who was banned from baseball for gambling, has served his time and should be inducted into Baseball's Hall of Fame.

Hey! Aren't We All Sinners?

To ban a player for life is ridiculous and is a case of double standards. I presume that the late Commissioner Giammati and the current commissioner, **Bud Selig**, are without blemish and have never sinned. Hog wash! One of the inductees, **Orlando Cepeda**, was charged with selling marijuana and has served time in jail. **Roberto Almar** spit in the face of an umpire and was fined a few dollars and given a 3 or 4 day suspension, only to return to baseball. **Darryl Strawberry**, whose drug problems continue as I write this, gets re-instated after each conviction. The afore mentioned players can't hold a candle to Pete Rose. Rose has the records and credentials (and thus my defense) for his position.

What is Bud Selig thinking? Rose only gambled, as so many Americans do each day in Las Vegas, Atlantic City, and the Indian casinos that are sprouting up all over the country. Maybe they are envious of Rose's hustle and ability. Whatever baseball is thinking; it is wrong. Rose had made amends, has confessed his sins (we're all sinners), and needs closure. In the meantime, Rose memorabilia is the hottest item for baseball enthusiasts. **What's that tell you?**

July 29, 1999   The Monterey County Post

Let the wine flow, we thought! When trying to open a wine-tasting room in Carmel, multiple restaurant owner, Farok Shield, was rebuked by the City Fathers (commission members).

Farok Shield owns Da Giovanni, Bistro Giovanni, and Beaujolais in the Carmel Plaza, all quality eating establishments catering to locals and tourists. He employs over forty-two workers to run the restaurants.

In addition to his love for the restaurants business, Mr. Shield has delved into wines...that is, cabernets, merlots, and zinfandels, all to compliment his restaurant cuisine. Farok Shield has become connoisseur and a wine expertise. He was to name his proposed wine-tasting room, Block 57 to coincide with his Bistro Giovanni, located on San Carlos Street in Carmel a few doors from his restaurant.

Mr. Shield adhered to all the rules and regulations, permits, etc. to get city approval and had passed all regulations twice. So, why was he finally turned down? A "walking tour" guide and would-be competitors who don't even live in Carmel, combined to convince the commission to turn Farok down. I thought "good and fair" competition is what our country is all about? Farok couldn't delay his prospective landlord anymore because the landlord was losing rental revenues, so he decided to give up the idea. He wrote a letter to that effect to Senior Planner Marc Wiener. Time, money and frustration was over.

We can only say that all his varietals (white and red) under the name of Block 57 have been blocked! That's how all the labels read. The council blew this one. Encourage business, not discourage, particularly those who employ many have a great reputation in the community. One consolation...all his great wines carry the name, Block 57.and are served in his restaurants.

Today, it's all about money, particularly in professional sports. The San Francisco Giants lost third baseman Pablo Sandavol to the Boston Red Sox and it was only a matter of a few dollars between the teams. Such is the case with many athletes who move from one club to another for more money.

Take the case of Hal Trosky, whose son, Lin Trosky is known in Carmel for his hair-cutting salon.

Hal Trosky became a sensational ball player with the Cleveland Indians in 1934 when he hit .330 with 35 homers and was paid $3,000 that year. How do you like that? Not only was he a great ball player, but he had the "Hollywood" looks. Some stories compared him with Errol Flynn, and others thought he would be more like Tarzan. He was called "Prince Hal," "Handsome Hal," and "Hoot"
Trosky's banner year was 1936 when he hit .342 with 42 home runs and knocked in 162 runs. That year, he made $7.500. It's ironic that Hal never made the All-Star team because his first-base competition was Hall of Famers, Gehrig, Jimmie Foxx, and Hank Greenberg.

Trosky drove in more than 100 runs in each of his first six seasons with the Indians and batting over .300 each year. His career ended abruptly because of excruciating headaches that tortured Trosky and he was forced to retire at the young age of 28. Word has it that he had those headaches from the time he was 16.

In the 50's Hal found a cure when he gave up eating and drinking dairy products and chewing tobacco. He was allergic to them, so says his son.

Can you imagine what his worth would be today in American sports? Probably 20 million a year. My how times have changed and today's athletes can take a lesson from their predecessors.

Why foreigners who emigrate to the United States have problems with English. Many words are pronounced the same but have different meanings. For example: The principal in the argument was devoid of moral principle. They propose to alter the place of the altar. He said the cymbal was a symbol of music. The stature of the statue of Liberty is fixed by statute. The able man's name was Abel. The horse with the long mane ran through the main street of Maine.

Are you confused? So am I!

Why major league baseball refuses to honor Pete Rose and his records is beyond belief. Sure, he gambled when he was managing the Cincinnati Reds baseball team but my question is, who hasn't gambled on sports?

We are barraged on television by all the Indian casinos and the Las Vegas casinos, locally and nationally, to entice people to visit them and gamble on the crap table or the slot machines. In California, the lotto is advertised constantly, here again, to get you folks to part with your money.

On golf courses, the pros (during practice rounds) gamble with each other to see who can play better and take the money home. In most towns in the United States, there are bingo parlors where players test their gambling skills (however the numbers come out) against the house.

I can go on and on, but I think you get the picture, whether it's Pete Rose or Joe Blow, gambling runs rampant in the United States and all over the world. We're all trying to hit the jackpot so to speak.

Pete Rose holds the hitting record in major league baseball and no one can take that away from him. Prior to his death, Commissioner Giammati handed down a life ban for Pete Rose, but now it's time for the new commissioner to rescind that edict. What's the saying, we've all sinned, so why can't we recognize the greatness of Pete Rose?

Since Rose was banned, countless players in baseball and football have gambled, killed, committed crimes of every nature. Rumor has it that John Daly, the golfer, lost thirty million dollars in Las Vegas. Has he been banned from playing golf? No! I can relate more indiscretions but why belabor the situation.

Pete Rose belongs in the Baseball Hall of Fame….his records have not been broken or tied. Remember, we are all sinners!

Being a baseball enthusiast for many years and an Oakland A's fan, going through my archives of writings, I came upon a verse or two regarding the top baseball team during the early 50's. That team was the Detroit Tigers.

I wrote the following epistle during my radio time at KREO in Indio, California. I tried to incorporate the player's names in the my musings. This type of writing goes back to my early days in the lower grades playing on words that would drive my teachers crazy with my rhyming. I thought it was clever but they didn't.

Maybe I was inspired to write in Indio because there wasn't much to do in that desert town during that period of time. Today, it's a thriving city, but in those days, it was a hot and dusty community.

Perhaps this was my way of keeping my mind active and thinking beyond the norm. To others it may seem incongruous and a bit on the stupid side. But if I can gain a chuckle or two from a friend of foe, it was well worth the effort.

So my advice to those creative minds, don't stop and go with the flow if you want to create something worthwhile, even a bit of writing:

Youth, speed, and stamina combine to make Red Rolfe's Raiders the pace setters in the Junior Circuit. The harmonious cries of the team members echo, Beat The Yankees. You might sum it all up in the following verse:

You know, it's Priddy fine to watch the Groth of any athletic organization...from rags to riches and from cellar dweller to league champions. Some query, Hou-te-men do it?? Well, it's simple! When skies are Gray and glum hovers with clubs on the diamond, those Tigers growl, Bring on the meat!! Arbiters smile when the Bengals play...you see, they make it a practice to give no Lip-on any particular play. What's Wertz (thank you Dizzy Dean) about other clubs is not taking this matter seriously...it's essential in winning games.

The Motor City Crew never Mull,en on any play...it's strictly Swift team work...an asset in the games-won column. We might mention that fans come from miles around in Trucks and cars to watch the Detroit nine make at it, and as is customary there are pros and cons in every crowd. Kell the ump they shout, or put Keller in to pinch hit!! Some yell vociferously...the result...an over-worked larynx and a White face.

At the season's conclusion, team members journey to their respective homes. Some may purchase a New-house, er enjoy the wonders of nature by indulging in Trout fishing.

And thus, we conclude a brief summary of why the Detroit Tigers are in first place in the American League. We extend our deepest regrets to those players neglected in this work of art. We use the term loosely.

P.S. Any similarity to Edgar Allen Poe is truly accidental, I assure you!

Sincerely,
Sam Salerno
Radio Station KREO
Indio, California,1950

AFTERWORD

All the stories and pictures in these previous pages comprise a summary of my ninety years from childhood in Pennsylvania and growing up in Los Angeles through my professional life in the media, mostly in Las Vegas and Monterey.

At this writing, I continue to be a member of the media, co-hosting a radio show with Dave Marzetti called *The Shagbag Show*, which is heard on Monterey radio station KION and streaming live on the Internet.

I know of no one except Vin Scully who, like me, is an octogenarian and still broadcasting, as I am. Oops, update: Now we are both nonogenarians, and Vin is retired from broadcasting,

I wrote this book feeling it would be useful to people considering careers in either broadcasting or writing. In broadcasting, I became an announcer, an engineer, program director, music director, sales manager, general manager, and finally, an owner. As a writer, I penned news stories, commentaries, short stories, press releases, and promotional pieces.

Yes, I did all of that, and maybe someone reading this will just shake their head, thinking "It can't be done." Well, it can be done, because I did it. I would recommend to anyone thinking about trying to do what I did, to consider this bit of advice: If I had it to do again, I would have specialized one, not two, different careers. I have to think it would have been easier to advance if I had focused on just one path.

The athletes and celebrities I came in contact with during my career were very friendly and cooperative, which made my job easier and more interesting. Today, unfortunately, it's more difficult to get interviews, pictures, etc., because most of them have agents, managers, and gurus who dictate what they do, who they talk to, and what they say.

Again, thanks for being interested in my story. I wish you luck in yours.

Sam Salerno

BOOKS FROM **SETONPUBLISHING.COM**

BY TONY SETON

Mokki's Peak

Silent Alarm

Deki-san

Equinox

No Soap, Radio

Paradise Pond

Selected Writings

The Brink

Jennifer

The Francie LeVillard Mysteries
    Volumes I-IX

Trinidad Head

Dead as a Doorbell

Just Imagine

Musings on Sherlock Holmes

The Autobiography of John Dough,
    Gigolo

Silver Lining

Mayhem

The Omega Crystal

Truth Be Told

13 Days of Fear

The Quality Interview / Getting it
    Right on Both Sides of the Mic

From Terror to Triumph /
    The Herma Smith Curtis Story

Don't Mess with the Press / How to
    Write, Produce, and Report Quality
    Television News

Right Car, Right Price

BY OTHER AUTHORS

Bedtime Stories for the Starving Romantic

Sam The Morning Man *Sam Salerno*

Hamilton & Egberta *Gerard Rose*

A Dog's Tale *Ron Wormser*

A Rich & Valued Life *Martin C. Needler*

The Enchanted Emerald *Donald Craghead*

The Dedicated Life of an American Soldier
    Ray Ramos

Life Is a Bumpy Road *Tony Albano*

From Hell to Hail Mary / A Cop's Story
    Frank DiPaola

From Colored Town to Pebble Beach: The
    Story of the Singing Sheriff *Pat DuVal*

The Early Troubles *Gerard Rose*

The Boy Captain *Gerard Rose*

Bless Me Father *Gerard Rose*

For I Have Sinned *Gerard Rose*

A Western Hero *Gerard Rose*

Red Smith in LA Noir *David Jones*

The Shadow Candidate *Rich Robinson*

Hustle is Heaven *Duncan Matteson*

Vision for a Healthy California *Bill Monning*

Three Lives of a Warrior *Phil Butler*

Live Better Longer *Hugh Wilson*

Green-Lighting Your Future / How You Can
    Manifest the Perfect Life *John Koeberer*

www.ingramcontent.com/pod-product-compliance
Lightning Source LLC
Chambersburg PA
CBHW041820090426

42811CB00009B/1054

9780998960500